Conventional Gestures

Meaning and Methodology

Richard L. Epstein

with the assistance and collaboration and illustrations by

Alex Raffi

Advanced Reasoning Forum

Advanced Reasoning Forum
P.O. Box 635
Socorro, NM 87801
(505) 835–2517
www.ARFbooks.org

ISBN   978-1-938421-24-2   hardback

ISBN   978-1-938421-25-9   e-book

When one thinks through thoroughly its descriptive, philosophical and archaeological parts and when one adds to these the practice of gesture, which can be found in all living nations, one sees how little is known of the power of gestural expression, and how much more there is to observe. But he who has never hesitated before the treacheries of the true Ocean, and who has never been terrified by it, should not allow this Ocean of knowledge to stop him. Courage then.

> Andrea de Jorio
> *La mimica degli antichi investigata nel gestire napoletano*

It's a swamp.

> Epstein

Acknowledgements

We wish to thank the following people whose generous assistance has helped us make this a better work:

Carolyn Kernberger, Melissa Axelrod, Sherman Wilcox,
Esperanza Buitrago Díaz, Troels Krøyer, Rogeria Gaudencio,
Signe Wolsgård Krøyer, Carmen Nocentelli, Lisa Leeper, and
Lynn Beene.

Conventional Gestures: Meaning and Methodology

Preface

In 1992 I was teaching English as a second language to foreign students in Cedar City, Utah. One day a Japanese student raised his hand to be called on—with his middle finger extended. I told him it wasn't a good idea to do that. He was puzzled. I explained that it was an obscenity, a direct challenge, and if he did it to someone on the street he might get his finger broken. He was glad to know. And I realized that my students couldn't recognize our most common gestures.

So I set out to make a list of those. I asked the other teachers at the school for their suggestions, giving them an idea of what I was looking for with a few examples. I compiled a list of 65 gestures. I described the movement of each gesture in words, in some cases with a little diagram, and gave a short explanation of the meaning of the gesture. This was adequate for use in our classes since we all knew the gestures. The other teachers were enthusiastic about the project, but there wasn't much more I could do because I couldn't illustrate the gestures.

In 1998 I was writing a textbook on critical thinking and was looking for a cartoonist to provide some illustrations. I met Alex Raffi, and we were able to develop over one hundred cartoons for that book. At the end of the project in 1999, I suggested to him that we work together to illustrate a book of common American gestures for students of English and for travelers to the United States.

It took a while for us to decide how we would illustrate the gestures. We needed to show the movement, but we quickly realized that without a context, the use and meaning of the gesture are unclear. So for each gesture we provided a context cartoon as well as a close-up illustration of just the movement. To that we added a telegraphic explanation of its meaning, just enough for a classroom or a tourist.

By observing and discussing with friends and colleagues, we compiled an illustrated draft with about 115 gestures. We showed that to acquaintances in the U.S. and in other countries. They suggested a few additional gestures, and the readers abroad commented on whether the illustrations were clear enough for them to recognize and duplicate. We had a couple offers at that time to publish it as a textbook for English-language classes, but we chose not to do so as no publisher was interested in marketing it to tourists as well.

Over the next several years I began to read more about gestures. I discussed gestures with colleagues in linguistics and philosophy. Alex Raffi and I asked our friends about gestures. We looked at other collections of gestures. We talked with Carolyn Kernberger about how women gesture in the United States. We began to observe more carefully people in daily life and in movies and television, looking for gestures we had missed. By 2003 we had a draft of this essay and an additional 120 gestures.

Still I felt there was much more to learn and puzzle out. I continued to read and to discuss the issues with Alex Raffi. I began talking with linguists at the University of New Mexico. But for the most part we put aside this project while I was writing books on logic and critical thinking and he was starting up a marketing company of which he was the artistic director.

We returned to the project in earnest in 2010. Working together, we completed a new draft of the gestuary with about 340 gestures, though less than half were illustrated. We found as we began compiling, indexing, and cross-referencing that we were less sure of what to include. Though we had begun with a clear idea of what we were trying to illustrate, namely, common American gestures, in order to decide what to include and to distinguish what we were studying from many other ideas of gesture, we had to be clearer about the criteria we had implicitly adopted. We also realized that to make general claims about gestures and to expand on the ideas we needed not just a list but illustrations for all of the gestures. We returned to our work, and now we have over 400 gestures in the gestuary.

We would like to complete that project, but we don't have the money. So we have decided to publish separately this book, which was meant as an introductory essay for the gestuary. Though Alex Raffi is an equal partner in making the gestuary, this work is principally by me, reflecting my concerns about meaning and methodology, and he should not be held responsible for any inaccuracies or mistakes here. We have made available the current draft of the gestuary on the website of the Advanced Reasoning Forum <www.AdvancedReasoningForum.org/gestures> so that the gestures whose names appear in italics in this text can be seen. We also intend to update there the Annotated Bibliography of this book as we receive information about new collections of gestures.

*   *   *   *   *   *   *

We begin here with an attempt to give explicit criteria for what we've included in the gestuary. Then we discuss how others have studied similar classes of gestures, comparing their methodology for compiling collections of gestures. With that as background we try to understand what and how a gesture means. Providing some categories of gestures leads to a better idea of the scope of our inquiry. After considering whether there are any universal gestures, and how gestures change over time, we discuss the difficulties in organizing a gestuary. We conclude with an annotated bibliography of collections of gestures that extends many of the discussions in the text.

I Gestures and Communication

A. Conventional gestures

In its widest use, the term "gesture" has been taken to cover almost all nonverbal behavior that someone can take as meaningful.[1]

We, however, take gestures to be a kind of non-verbal *communication*. Though we may infer from someone blushing that she is embarrassed, she does not do it to communicate with us: the blushing is a sign that she is embarrassed.[2] When we see dark clouds lowering over a mountain, we infer that it will rain there; the clouds are a sign that it will rain; there is no communication.

To distinguish between communications and signs, we might invoke intentions: when I wave hello I intend for you to understand an idea I am trying to convey; when I blush I do not do so with the intention of you understanding my mood; and clouds have no intentions at all. But there are big problems in relying on intentions as a defining characteristic of communication. It is often difficult for an observer to discern an intention. Yet unless we can clearly do so, and unless the person is consciously aware of his or her intention, then waving hello would not be different in this respect from blushing: we infer the intention along with the meaning.

Rather, *communications, as opposed to signs, are based on a learned, shared system of acts we do that we deem to be symbolic*. Such acts might be speech, or writing, or movements, or postures, or markers left by a road, or anything else a particular group takes to be part of its system. By this criterion, clouds do not communicate because clouds don't learn; only sentient creatures learn. This also excludes physical reactions that we cannot control, such as blushing, for they, too, are not learned. Yes, we learn to understand the significance of acts like blushing or a trembling hand, but the person who does them does not learn to do them to *convey an idea beyond the act itself*, which is what we mean by an act being *symbolic*. When we see someone hitting another person, we know that the person who is striking out is angry, but the hitting is not symbolic of that: it's just hitting, a consequence of the person's anger, from which we can infer the anger; hitting someone is not part of our symbolic system. By focusing on a shared symbolic system, we substitute an *intersubjective* criterion for communication for the entirely subjective one of intentions.[3]

Communication, then, requires three parts:

A symbolic system agreed upon by a group.
A person who uses some part of that system.
A person who understands that part.

---

[1] See the scope of the articles in the journal *Gestures*.

[2] Betty J. Baüml and Franz H. Baüml, *A Dictionary of Gestures*, p. 56, call blushing a gesture.

[3] See Epstein, Fred Kroon, and William S. Robinson, "Reasoning with Subjective Claims," 2013, for an explanation of what is meant by subjective and intersubjective criteria.

Communication is not solely in the eye of the beholder.[4] When we say that the symbolic system is agreed upon by a group, we do not mean that the agreements need be explicit or that every person who uses the system was consciously aware of learning the symbolic value of each part. When we learn to speak and adopt the symbolic system of our language, we do so by imitation more than by conscious appreciation of symbolic acts.

We understand a dog pushing her food dish insistently to her master to be trying to communicate to him that she wants to be fed. That is learned behavior, which both the dog and her master understand. By our definition, which does not take intentions into account, it is an act of communication. But to extend our study to include dogs, horses, donkeys, and more would be too much. We'll confine our investigation to human communication. So now we have restricted our studies to:

- Human nonverbal communication: nonverbal human acts that are a part of a learned, shared system of acts that some group of people deem to be symbolic.

When someone leaves stones in the form of an arrow in a forest along one side of a fork in a trail, that's an act of communication. But it may be days or even years before anyone reads that message. Let's leave aside such static signals to consider only communication that is done more or less immediately, without a delay between the act of communicating and when another person is expected to understand.

---

[4] Compare what Paul Ekman and Wallace V. Friesen say in "Nonverbal Behavior in Psychotherapy," 1968:

> The term *communicate* refers to the fact that observers are able reliably to decode information from viewing a sample of nonverbal behavior. There is no implication that the person enacting the nonverbal behavior intended to communicate nor any assumption that the communication is necessarily accurate. p. 186

Morton Wiener, Shannon Devoe, Stuart Rubinow, and Jesse Geller in "Nonverbal Behavior and Nonverbal Communication," 1972, explain the importance of distinguishing between signs and communication in the study of nonverbal behavior:

> Investigators who share this perspective also appear to share an assumption that if the observer can make an inference about an individual from his behavior, then the behavior can be considered to be a communication. Unfortunately, this kind of implicit assumption seems to fuse the notion of sign with the notion of communication. For us, "sign" implies only an observer making an inference from, or assigning some significance to, an event or behavior, while "communication" implies (*a*) a socially shared signal system, that is, a code, (*b*) an encoder who makes something public via that code, and (*c*) a decoder who responds systematically to that code. p. 186

> If no distinction is made between signs and communications, it is unclear how such an approach could contribute anything to the study of communication as a special system or as a special set of behaviors. In fact, there seems to be no logical basis for excluding from communication instances of any occurrence about which the observer might make an inference. p. 190

- The form of communication is normally done in the presence of someone who could understand it more or less immediately.

A mute person could put down stones in the form of an arrow for someone standing next to her to see, and if she were to do such acts regularly and her companion understood them, then that would qualify under this restriction, too. What counts as normal depends on the group that shares the system of communication.

When we speak in the United States, we often use a chopping motion with our hand and forearm to provide emphasis for what we're saying. Motions like this that we make to accompany speech are important in facilitating communication, but without speech they are (nearly) meaningless. Let's leave those aside to focus on what is more strictly nonverbal.

- The communication can be understood without any accompanying speech, even though words or sounds might often accompany the act and even though that kind of act might at times accompany speech.

A mime on a street corner or a worker pretending to hammer a nail to get someone to bring her a hammer are meant to communicate at that moment without any speech. If we include all such kinds of acting and pantomime, we'll have to survey all that's taught in acting schools. But on what basis are we to distinguish someone pretending to hammer from someone waving hello (*Hello*) as a form of communication? The woman pretending to hammer might just as well intend to communicate that the other person should bring her some nails or that he should next start hammering. Even in a quite particular kind of context what we infer from her movement could be wrong. In contrast, waving hello is a regular part of the repertoire of a large group that uses it with a regular, conventional, standard meaning. That also distinguishes waving hello from someone acting like a bear by standing more than erect with her hands like claws at either side of her head while growling; though most of us would act similarly if intending to convey the idea of a bear, it is not part of our usual repertoire of communication, and we feel when we do it that we're improvising. Let's exclude such communications from our study by being clearer about what we mean by a symbolic value for an act.

- The form of communication has for the group that uses it a regular, conventional, standard meaning, where that meaning may depend on one or a few kinds of context.

Note that by this criterion a gesture has one standard meaning. A single *symbolic movement* that has two distinct meanings depending on context counts as two gestures according to this criterion.

A person who stands still while all around her are running around in panic conveys that she is unperturbed, that she is in command of her emotions. So it seems that standing still while others are running around satisfies the criteria we've adopted. But in a different context standing still might indicate patience, and in another context it might mean indecision about what to do. Lack of movement doesn't have a regular, standardized meaning, even relative to specified contexts. However, in some contexts it does. When someone offers another person his hand for a handshake, and the other person does not extend his hand in return, we understand that as an insult, an unwillingness to acknowledge the person who is extending his hand. Lack of movement when a response is normally expected to either a gesture or an initiation of a gesture often has a regular, clearly understood symbolic value. So we adopt the following criterion.

- The form of communication involves movement or else is a lack of movement in response to a form of non-verbal communication that normally requires a particular kind of movement in response.

When a woman goes to the main aisle leading to the altar in a Catholic church and crosses herself, many people in the United States would understand what she means. There are many such rituals associated with groups large enough to have influence on most Americans. But to study all rituals is too much for us here.

- The communication is not part of a ritual.

This is not meant to exclude gestures of superstition, particular for good or bad luck, though the line between ritual and generally-held superstition may be difficult to draw.

In summary, the following criteria determine what we mean by ***conventional gestures***:

- Human nonverbal communication: nonverbal human acts that are a part of a learned, shared system of acts that some group of people deem to be symbolic.

- The form of communication is normally done in the presence of someone who can understand it more or less immediately.

- The communication can be understood without any accompanying speech, even though words or sounds might often accompany the act and even though that kind of act may at times accompany speech.

- The form of communication has for the group that uses it a regular, conventional, standard meaning, where that meaning may depend on one or a few kinds of context.

- The form of communication involves movement or else is a lack of movement in response to a form of non-verbal communication that normally requires a particular kind of movement in response.

- The communication is not part of a ritual.

In the annotated bibliography you can find discussions of collections of gestures from many different countries and cultures, each different from the others. Even within the general culture of the United States, there are groups such as the old Hispanic communities in northern New Mexico and the ultra-orthodox Jewish communities in New York that have different ways of communicating nonverbally. People who lived in the United States a hundred years ago had a different culture, and there is no reason to think that they had the same system of nonverbal communication as ours. Before we can generalize about nonverbal systems of communication, we need examples of particular ones adopted by particular groups. For our studies here we'll focus our attention on conventional gestures that also satisfy the following criterion:

- Nonverbal communication that is part of the general culture of the United States at the time this book is written: most Americans now would recognize and understand the form of communication, even if they might not typically use it themselves.

We call such forms of communication *American conventional gestures*. In this essay we sometimes use the term "conventional gestures" for American conventional gestures when we're not comparing them to gestures of other cultures. Indeed, we often use the term "gesture" as shorthand for "American conventional gesture," trusting to context to make that clear.

B. Conventional gestures compared to some other nonverbal behavior
In order to clarify the scope of our subject, we'll consider whether some particular kinds of nonverbal behavior are conventional gestures.

1. Wearing apparel and how we present ourselves
When a woman goes to work in a suit rather than her usual blouse and slacks, she is indicating to those she meets that she should be taken more seriously than usual. When someone wears a gold ring on the third finger of her left hand, we understand that to mean she is married.

These are forms of communication and they satisfy all our criteria except one: they are not immediate, unless we count all the time a person is wearing a wedding ring as the duration of the act, which might be the rest of her life. These are not conventional gestures.

2. Body language
When we stand talking to someone, we adjust the space between ourselves. Though we often sense that there is a meaningful difference between standing so close that we can smell each others' breath and standing more than an arm's length from someone, we would be hard-pressed to say what that difference is. As one of us moves closer, the other may move a bit further away without any thought by either that some idea has been conveyed by those movements. Though we learn how to

adjust the distance between ourselves, and though an observer might be able to discern the significance of such movements, we ourselves do not consider them part of our system of communication. We do not consider ourselves to be employing part of a symbolic system when we move closer or further. We call **body language** movements and postures that we adopt from which others can infer meaning but which we do not ourselves normally consider to be part of our symbolic system of nonverbal communication.[5] Body language, then, is outside the scope of the study of conventional gestures.[6]

3. Communicative postures

Closely related to body language are certain static postures we adopt that we do consider to be part of our system of communication; these we call **communicative postures**. It takes no trained observer to know that when someone is standing quietly with his hands on his hips, he's thinking or doesn't want to be disturbed (*Arms akimbo-thinking*). Though the line between these and body language is difficult to draw, we include some of them in our gestuary.

4. Communicating with oneself

Though our notion of conventional gesture is grounded in the idea of communication, there need not be another person to whom a gesture is directed. It's not unusual to see someone hit his head with his open palm to indicate that he has realized he's made an error (*Blast!–head slap*) even though no one else is nearby. Just as talking to oneself is talking, so conventional gestures done only for oneself are conventional gestures.

5. Objects used in nonverbal communication

When in a heated discussion with a man, a woman picks up a frying pan and holds it at shoulder level as if to strike, she is communicating that she is mad. Some

---

[5] That much body language does not have standard meaning is evident from the often fanciful interpretations given to it. For example, F. Kostolany in *Los Gestos*, 1977, p. 58, says that "gestures which tend to be oriented to the right . . . will be not only an index of generosity and openness ("entrega"), but also of prodigality and vanity."

[6] Compare Adam Kendon in de Jorio, *Gesture in Naples and Gesture in Classical Antiquity*, 1832/2000, p. xix:

> "Gesture", that is, visible bodily action that is considered to be a part of a person's willful expression.
>
>   footnote: A degree of voluntarism always seems implied, and, generally speaking, expressions such as laughing or crying, blushing and the like, are not considered "gestures" unless, perhaps, as is sometimes the case, they can be feigned. Gesticulations that are part of spoken utterance, the use of manual gestures to convey something when speech is impossible, the manual and facial actions of sign languages are all, undeniably, "gesture". Changes in posture or the assumption of one posture or another, though often "expressive" and "voluntary" are not generally considered "gesture" although in some circumstances this may be appropriate.

movements in our shared system of communication involve objects that we manipulate or touch. There are many objects we use, but since we often use just whatever comes to hand, such uses would not be regular enough to count as conventional gestures. Still, some uses of objects are so standardized, so part of our usual repertory, such as *Knocking on a door*, *Knock on wood*, and *Tapping a glass for attention*, that we can count them as conventional. In particular, we include those that involve some part of the gesturer's wearing apparel, such as *Tip of the hat*.

6. *Stylized emotions*

We use the term **stylized emotion** for any standardized movement that indicates an emotion or state of the body that might not typically be used to communicate, even though it can be interpreted easily by an observer. For example, a person might hug herself when cold. An analogue in spoken language to a gesture that is a stylized emotion would be uttering "Ouch" when in pain. A. G. Bills in *General Experimental Psychology*, 1934, says:

> Most overt expression is sooner or later used for communication of meaning, as a sort of language, through which individuals convey their moods to others. On this account the overt expression is sure to become conventionalized and exaggerated in conformance to certain social concepts.

L. Carmichael, S. O. Roberts, and N. Y. Wessell in "Study of the Judgment of Manual Expression as Presented in Still and Motion Pictures," 1937, respond to Bills:

> The opposite viewpoint holds that, nevertheless, a core of basic reaction patterns independent of learning exists, which is itself sufficiently differential to permit the identification of separate "emotions." p. 133

But the two viewpoints are not necessarily opposed. An emotion could be expressed in a range of ways, all of which we could usually identify, though only one of those, perhaps in an exaggerated form, is typically used in a particular society.[7] For example, Laurence Wylie in *Beaux Gestes: A Guide to French Body Talk*, 1977, says:

> Why does a French child shake his finger to express pain or the premonition of pain? I do not know whether this is a spontaneous body reaction or whether children learn the gesture through imitation of adults. In any case, to shake the

---

[7] But Mary Key, "Gestures and Responses: A Preliminary Study Among Some Indian Tribes of Bolivia," 1962, reporting on contact with previously isolated tribes in Bolivia (annotated below), suggests that the expression of emotions may be so culturally determined as to be unintelligible to someone from another culture. Robert G. Harper, Arthur N. Wiens, and Joseph D. Matarazzo, *Nonverbal Communication: The State of the Art*, 1978, particularly pp. 77–78 and p. 99, have a review of literature on the question of whether there are universal facial expressions of emotions. Compare also the discussion by Kendon in Section 3.4 of the Introduction to de Jorio, 1832/2000.

> hand so that the fingers flap together is the usual French expression for reaction
> to pain. p. 55

In the United States we do not normally indicate that we are in pain or have a
premonition of pain in this way, though we sometimes do. Rather, we grimace:
mouth stretched as wide as possible and slightly down, brow furrowed down, eyes
closed or nearly closed. We suspect many French people grimace with pain at times.
But we, as they, have chosen one of many physiological reactions to pain to be the
standard we use, both to convey that we feel pain when we wish to communicate
that, and, after long habituation, as our usual unconscious reaction to pain.

Is a stylized emotion a conventional gesture? That depends on whether it is
symbolic. *A sufficient condition for a nonverbal act to be symbolic is that someone
from another group or culture cannot understand it without an explanation.* For
example, we were undecided whether *Ohhh–contentment*—where someone leans
back after a meal and pats his belly—was just a physical reaction/stylized emotion
or a conventional gesture, until a friend from Colombia asked us what it meant.
Obviously, we thought, it means we're content; so it must be symbolic.

Decisions about whether each stylized emotion is a conventional gestures are
too much for us to engage in here. We include in our gestuary only a few that we
think are often used to communicate.

7. *Speech markers*

Speech markers are those movements we make that accompany speech and that are
meant to facilitate verbal communication. Done without the appropriate speech, they
are (nearly) meaningless; hence, they are not conventional gestures.

Adam Kendon in "Gestures," 1987, uses another term for apparently the same
class of movements.

> The term "gesticulation" is used to refer to bodily movements which often are
> observed to accompany speech and which, even to a casual observer, are seen to
> be patterned in relation to it. These movements are usually considered to be part
> of a speaker's total expression. p. 462

The term *illustrators* is sometimes used for these kind of gestures that depict
or point out, while *gesticulation* is used by others for all kinds of non-verbal
communication that involves movement.

Albert E. Scheflen in "The Significance of Posture in Communication
Systems," 1964, notes:

> Every American speaker generally raises his head slightly at the end of
> statements to which he expects an answer. He does so because all other
> Americans recognize this postural form for eliciting an answer.[8]

---

[8] p. 318. Scheflen points out that speech markers have analogues in speech:

> It is well known in structural linguistics that the unit known as the syntactic sentence is
> marked by a terminal change in pitch. These "markers" are called junctures. There are

Scheflen's use of "because" suggests speakers use speech markers consciously, though that seems unlikely to us. Speech markers need not be performed only by the person speaking. For example, in the United States it's common to continue to nod your head while listening to someone to encourage him or her to continue speaking.

Joe Stephenson, Nancy Pine, Zhang Liwei, and Xie Xian in "Some Gestures Commonly Used in Nanjing, PRC," 1995, distinguish speech markers from a class like conventional gestures by the criterion of being able to recall using them:

> The gestures described here are those which are or can be used independent of speech, and which have a generally agreed upon symbolic meaning that is fairly specific. . . . Gestures are distinct from gesticulations or other hand, facial, or body movements that accompany speech, and are sometimes called "illustrators". Gesticulations are for the most part unconscious. A speaker will not be able to recall the gesticulations that accompanied his or her speech, but will frequently be able to recall the gestures that were used in nonverbal interaction. p. 236

But often we cannot remember what conventional gesture we've used when queried, and others we've spoken to say the same. Conventional gestures are part of our method of communicating, of which we are not always fully aware. Conscious use, in the sense of planning and/or remembering what we do, is difficult to attribute to our ordinary speaking. We often find it hard to remember exactly what we said a moment ago or even roughly what we said two moments ago. Most of us, most of the time, do not plan what we are going to say; we just talk. Indeed, there is no planning of what is to be said short of having an internal conversation with oneself, which as a criterion of conscious use would lead to an infinite regress. The use of verbal language, no less than the use of conventional gestures, is spontaneous and often not something we remember. Requiring that a movement be planned or can be remembered is not part of the criteria for whether a movement is a conventional gesture.[9]

One might try to distinguish between speech markers and conventional gestures by asking whether someone could understand the meaning of the movement from a

three types in English: A rise in pitch, indicating a question; a fall in pitch, indicating completion; and a holding of pitch, indicating the speaker will continue. p. 320

Scheflen says on p. 316 without any explanation, "We estimate that there are no more than about thirty traditional American gestures."

[9] Wiener, Devoe, Rubinow, and Geller, 1972, say:

> We assume further that the relationship between behavior A and experience X, for a particular communication group, must at the start of the relationship between A and X (or in developing any formal code) have been made with some awareness, although the experience of self-conscious use of A to stand for X may dissipate for the group as well as for the individual with increasing association of A with X. That is, we view this shift to nonawareness as being no different than the equivalent change in awareness in driving a car. . . . We hold that the self-consciousness involved in communicative behaviors is evident only for relatively inexperienced communicators. p. 203–204

soundless video of it. But a soundless video showing a man at a meeting with others around a table who hits the table with his palm will be understood by Americans to mean that he is giving emphasis. We understand the meaning of the movement, but we don't know what he is giving emphasis to; for that we need the sound, and such a movement is normally made only with speech. The movement is a speech marker, not a conventional gesture.

8. Illustrative gestures

Communicative movements that are not regularly employed with the same recognized meaning, such as pretending to hammer a nail, we call **illustrative gestures**; others suggest calling them *charades* or *pantomimes*. Such gestures may be highly dependent on context to understand. They are idiosyncratic in the sense that the person making them is not copying a conventional gesture, a standard way to communicate, even though the gesture might not be idiosyncratic in the sense that it is used by only this one person or that this person imbues the movement with a significance that others do not. Illustrative gestures are not conventional gestures.

We have not tried here to develop a typology of nonverbal communications. Our goal is to clarify the scope of what we're investigating. We agree with Kendon who says in *Gestures*, 2004:

> Gestures cannot be pinned down into a typology in any fixed way. The distinctions and classifications that are unavoidably created whenever it is discussed reflect the different understandings that students of gesture have had of how it functions. The particular classification systems developed are useful working instruments for a given investigation, but they should not be thought of as more than this. pp. 84–85

II   The Methodology of Identifying Conventional Gestures

We need a catalogue of American conventional gestures before we can begin to analyze them. How we go about cataloguing them will determine to some extent what observations we are likely to make. In this section we discuss two methods used to identify and catalogue classes of gestures similar to conventional ones that we then compare to our approach.

A. Saitz and Cervenka

Robert L. Saitz and Edward Cervenka in *Handbook of Gestures: Colombia and the United States*, 1962/1972, compare American and Colombian gestures. They say:

> This study . . . focuses on gestures which (1) seem discrete (that is they have an essential physical movement which, informants agree, characterizes the gesture), and (2) are easily recognizable by an untrained observer. Actually, of course, most of what we here call gestures are complexes of motions, analogous perhaps to the larger units of linguistic communication, such as the sentence, which are capable of being analyzed further into discrete components. . . . Our purpose in using the larger unit recognized as 'gesture' here has been to collect a corpus or loci, to gather together as many gesture complexes as possible and to designate them with a broad semantic label (which calls attention to an area of meaning that the complex be associated with), as a stimulus to further research. We have excluded, for the most part, some specialized gesture systems which merit collection and study: (1) the difficult to see (but certainly significant) changes in pupil openings, and in the movement of minute facial muscles; (2) ritual gesture systems used within relatively closed groups (church, army, sports . . .); (3) deaf and dumb systems; (4) children's game gestures; (5) heavily iconic gestures (a child's imitation of driving a car, . . . , fingers closing to depict a scissors, etc.); (6) stage gestures; (7) paralanguage. pp. 7–8

It appears that Saitz and Cervenka are studying a class of gestures the same as or very similar to conventional ones.

They describe their method:

> We collected the gestures of the Colombians on the basis of personal observations in Colombia during 1960–1962 and from interviews with Colombian informants during the same period. The interviews with the Colombian informants, two male and two female, took place over a period of twelve months and consisted of (1) our presentation of observed gestures for their recognition and comment, and (2) discussion and simulation of varied contexts in an attempt to elicit further gestures. During the same period and afterwards, some twenty informants, male and female, from different regions of the U.S., were interviewed by the same procedures. To the gestures collected and published in 1962, we have added others for this edition, collected through our own observation and through the response of readers to the initial publication. . . .

The informants from the U.S. represented a wide range of ages and geographical and social backgrounds. pp. 7–8

In the first published version of their work the gestures were drawn by Renee Bigio; those were replaced by illustrations by Mel Pekarsky for the 1972 edition.

B. Johnson, Ekman, and Friesen

In "Communicative Body Movements: American Emblems," 1975, Harold G. Johnson, Paul Ekman, and Wallace V. Friesen compiled a list of about 100 American gestures they call *emblems*.

> There need not be concomitant speech or any verbal conversation at all, although emblems can and do occur during conversation. . . .
> Emblems differ from most other bodily movements or facial expressions in that the person observing the emblem, the decoder, assumes that the action was performed deliberately by the actor or encoder to provide the decoder with a message. The encoder typically acknowledges he is communicating; he usually takes responsibility for what he transmits, much as he would with his words. p. 336

This sounds like the kind of gestures we are considering. But then they quote an earlier paper by Ekman and Friesen:

> Emblems are those nonverbal acts (a) which have a direct verbal translation usually consisting of a word or two, or a phrase, (b) for which this precise meaning is known by most or all members of a group, class, subculture or culture, (c) which are most often deliberately used with the conscious intent to send a particular message to the other person(s), (d) for which the person(s) who sees the emblem usually not only knows the emblem's message but also knows that it was deliberately sent to him, and (e) for which the sender usually takes responsibility for having made that communication. A further touchstone of an emblem is whether it can be replaced by a word or two, its message verbalized without substantially modifying the conversation.[10]

Ekman and Friesen in "The Repertoire of Nonverbal Behavior: Categories, Origins, Usage, and Coding," 1969, also say:

> Emblems are those nonverbal acts which have a direct verbal translation, or dictionary definition, usually consisting of a word or two, or perhaps a phrase. . . .

> An emblem may repeat, substitute, or contradict some part of the concomitant verbal behavior; a crucial question in detecting an emblem is whether it could be replaced with a word or two without changing the information conveyed. p. 63

But they then stress that there need not be concomitant verbal behavior:

> Emblems occur most frequently where verbal exchange is prevented by noise, external circumstance, . . . p. 64

---

[10] Ekman and Friesen, "Hand Movements", 1972, p. 357.

None of these criteria serve to exclude illustrative gestures. But in "Communicative Body Movements: American Emblems," 1975, Johnson, Ekman, and Friesen say:

> Take the example of the message "hammering a nail into the wall." If people are asked how to transmit this message, they will usually perform a similar motor action, involving a hammering movement with one hand while the other hand holds an invisible nail. If the informants followed our instruction to provide only actions they had seen in normal conversation, not pantomimes or charades, they would not make such an invention. p. 339

The gestures they consider, then, are ones that can be used in place of verbal communication.

The requirement that a gesture has a short verbal equivalent seems to restrict attention to a narrower class than our conventional gestures. As we discuss in Section III, for some conventional gestures it is difficult to find an adequate translation into verbal language, much less a short verbal equivalent. But it is impossible to be sure what Johnson, Ekman, and Friesen intend since they give only the names or verbal equivalents of the American gestures they collected with no description of the movements involved. Considering how both the meaning and form of gestures change over time and are dependent on context (Section VI and Section III.B below), we are unsure which if any of the gestures in our gestuary correspond to ones in their list.[11] Or perhaps they are studying American conventional gestures but believe that all of those have a short verbal equivalent.

In their paper they describe the methodology they used to collect gestures:

> Simply asking people to perform the emblems they knew (once explaining the definition of an emblem) was unproductive. People remembered few. On the other hand, if people were read a list of messages and asked if they had an emblem for each message, it was easy for them to recall and perform emblems they knew. Importantly, this procedure also seemed to stimulate memory since informants frequently would volunteer emblems not on the list of messages read to them.
>
> The message list utilized in this study included the list developed by Ekman and Friesen for use in Japan and the Fore in New Guinea. It included all emblems found for those two groups and many messages not emblems for either. Messages which were reported as emblems by Efron [1941/1972] and Saitz and Cervenka [1962/1972] were also included. ...
>
> Each informant was queried individually, with the entire procedure recorded on videotape. The investigator was very careful not to provide suggestions (verbal or nonverbal). Frequently he paused to ask the informant to volunteer emblems or alternate ways to convey the same message.

---

[11] The authors say in their paper that they plan to publish a video record of the gestures, but Ekman (private communication) has told us that the video was never made public and is now unavailable.

Since emblems might vary with age, sex, ethnic background, or social class a homogenous pool of informants was selected for this initial survey in the United States. The informants selected were white, middle-class males between the ages of 21 and 35 years, at least third-generation United States, and living in an urban setting.

The performances of fifteen informants were videotaped. It is difficult to determine how many informants to use in a study such as this. The decision was made to stop when the informants did not volunteer any new items. After the tenth subject, only one or two new emblems were volunteered and it seemed reasonable to assume that we had exhausted what could be learned about the emblem repertoire using this procedure.[12]

Johnson, Ekman, and Friesen explain how they then analyzed the data:

The visual analysis of the emblem performances to determine similarity did not involve precise measurement. Instead the assessment was a global judgment performed by the first author, and partially verified by the other authors. Decisions about similarity did not seem difficult. It seemed obvious that either the performances were minor variations on a particular action pattern, or they were markedly different in appearance. One hundred and thirty-eight motor patterns met the criterion of visual similarity. This did not mean, however, that all 138 actions were necessarily emblems, but only that most people performed the same action for each of these messages. p. 339

The third part of their method is "decoding": showing videotapes of the gestures to subjects to see if the subjects produce the same message for the gesture and whether they consider the gesture to be an emblem or an "artificial" gesture, that is, a kind of pantomime. A movement is then classified as an emblem on the basis of a high enough percentage of informants classifying it as an emblem and reproducing its message. Verified emblems require at least 70% of the decoders to match the message correctly and judge the pattern "natural"; probable emblems require at least 70% of the decoders to match the message correctly, but only between 50% and 70% to judge the gesture natural; ambiguous emblems require only 50% to 70% to match the message and judge the gesture natural. When less than 50% of the decoders agreed on the message, the gesture was not considered further.

C. Problems with messages and with collecting gestures as an anthropological or psychological study

The approach of Johnson, Ekman, and Friesen seems disingenuous to us. They weren't studying natives of a different culture. Each of the emblems they found should have been familiar to them from their daily lives. If one of those emblems

---

[12] pp. 337–338. Ekman and Friesen, "The Repertoire of Nonverbal Behavior: Categories, Origins, Usage, and Coding", 1969, pp. 66–68, discuss how they originally used this method to study emblems of the Fore in New Guinea, though it appears they have not published a list of the gestures they collected there nor made available the films they say they made.

wasn't familiar, the informant could have explained what it meant. By way of comparison, no one thinks it appropriate to compile a dictionary of words by making noises and finding if informants come up with the same messages for them. Among other reasons, we would have great difficulty in deciding if two sounds were "sufficiently similar" if we did not already know what we were listening for.[13] It should have been easy for the authors to make judgments of similarity of motor actions since they were familiar with most if not all of the gestures.

The third part of their method was "decoding." But the authors should have been able to make those judgments since they were native speakers of the gestures. In any case, we do not say that an action is not a gesture because someone or a lot of people don't understand it, any more than we would say that "exogenous" is not a word because few informants have any idea what it means and would classify it as a nonsense sound. Their investigation at best could determine whether a movement is a common gesture, not whether it is a gesture. In comparison, we know some gestures that we don't include in our gestuary because we think they are not common enough.[14]

A colleague in Brazil wrote us after studying the first draft of our little book of gestures for students of English that she had seen a gesture in American movies that we had not included and she was curious what it meant. One person holds his fist in front of his body, sticks out his forefinger, and asks the other person to pull it, who does just that. We had to explain to her that this was a joke, not a gesture: the person who offers his finger will fart when his finger is pulled. As native speakers of American gestures, we can recognize the difference between a gesture and a joke. We need to know the gesture before we can recognize it as a gesture.

A more serious problem with the method of Johnson, Ekman, and Friesen is the ambiguity of what they mean by "message," which we discuss more fully in Section III.A. Consider what they say:

> Many messages are emblematic in more than one culture, but a different movement is used in each culture. . . . For example, in the U.S. the emblem for suicide is placing the hand to the temple, with the hand in the "gun-shooting" emblem position (index finger extended, thumb raised and moved towards and away from the index finger, and the other fingers curled into the palm). In the Fore of New Guinea the emblem for suicide is grabbing the throat with an open hand and pushing up, a representation of hanging, which is how these people commit suicide. In Japan the suicide emblem is either to plunge one fist into the stomach, a representation of hari-kari, or to draw the index finger across the neck, a representation of slitting the throat.[15]

---

[13] This is the analogous to the problem of identifying phonemic structure in another language as C. F. Hockett discusses in *Refurbishing our Foundations*, 1987.

[14] For example, Epstein thought that *Thumbs down* followed by rotating the thumb as if squashing a bug to indicate that an idea, person, or situation was (or should be) rubbed out (fully eliminated) was common, but we now think it's archaic or at least not well-known.

[15] Ekman and Friesen, "Hand Movements," 1972, p. 365.

What is wrong here, besides noting that the last movement they describe is also used in the U.S., is that in the U.S. the gesture they describe does not mean "suicide."[16] It is difficult to find a verbal equivalent to that gesture (*Shooting oneself in the head*), but it cannot be a single word. Generally, a verbal equivalent of a gesture must be a complete sentence or a description of an emotion to be conveyed or elicited. The gun-shooting gesture in the U.S. means something like, "I just realized that I made a stupid mistake, so stupid that I might as well have just shot myself in the head." It is used figuratively. Starting with a preconceived list of messages for subjects to demonstrate may give an incorrect interpretation of a gesture. Furthermore, their method does not take into account the context in which the emblem is appropriate, which may be crucial in determining its meaning, as we discuss in Section III.B.

To illustrate the problems their methodology creates when the author is not a native speaker of the gestures, consider the study of Persian (Iranian) emblems carried out in Tehran, in Michigan, and in New York (1976) by an American, Carol Magda Pearson Sparhawk. She says,

> During the decoding phase, when an informant failed to identify an emblem I presented, I would tell him or her which message I had expected. He (she) would then correct my performance if necessary. As one informant commented that she recognized the emblem I performed, I had an 'accent', but the performances on the whole must have been recognizable.[17]

Similarly, she concocts strings for her informants to decode, which they can, but that tells us nothing about whether they would perform them; such sequences may simply have the status of pantomime. Looking at her illustrated list of gestures, we cannot be sure that all of the entries are conventional gestures or emblems, nor that the "message" is correct. For example, we find "Suicide" (p. 196) illustrated as raising the hand in the shape of a gun to the head as if shooting oneself in the head, which is the "message" that Johnson, Ekman, and Friesen give for Americans and which we know is incorrect, though it may be one of the movements you'll get if you give that message to someone.

We think that Johnson, Ekman, and Friesen, 1975, are wrong when they say:

> This report describes a method of identifying the emblem repertoire for any group, literate or preliterate, which is usable with people once they reach the age where they comprehend language. p. 337

---

[16] According to Bruno Munari, *Supplemento al Dizionario Italiano* (English translation *Speak Italian*, 1963/2002, p. 66) the slitting the throat movement is identified as a threat in Italy. Luc Nisset in *French in Your Face*, 2007, has the following phrases for it: "It's over! It's done! He's done for! Keep quiet! Shut up! (cutting throat) • They went bankrupt!" (p. 148). Hamiru•aqui in *70 Japanese Gestures*, 2004, p. 103, says "This gesture is used when talking about someone that has been fired."

[17] Sparhawk, *Linguistics and Gesture: An Application of Linguistic Theory to the Study of Persian Emblems*, 1976, p. 28. See also Sparhawk, "Contrastive-Identification Features of Persian Gesture," 1978.

Ekman later wrote:

> The size of the repertoire of emblems varies quite considerably among the groups we have studied. The smallest seems to be the middle-class Americans with less than 100 and the largest the Israeli students with more than 250. We should note that the methods described may miss some emblems, but we believe they should uncover most emblems.[18]

We have no reason to believe that Americans employ significantly more emblems now than in 1976, which suggests that their methodology missed more than two-thirds of American conventional gestures, though perhaps not all of those would qualify as emblems.

The study of gestures by someone treating it as a psychology experiment or anthropological investigation is going to lack the crucial identification of movements *as* conventional gestures that only a native speaker can provide. The project of compiling a gestuary is much the same as compiling a dictionary. We already know the gestures, and we may miss some in our first attempt at making a list, but consulting colleagues, friends, other collections, and other sources should suffice. No single experiment can substitute for the long task of watching, and remembering, and discussing, and tracking down as many conventional gestures as we native speakers can find.

Further, Johnson, Ekman, and Friesen do not do the fundamental work needed for a reputable psychology experiment: their protocol is not clearly enough stated for someone to try to replicate their work; and with only the "messages" of the gestures listed with no description of the movements nor video recordings available, even if someone could replicate the experiment, it wouldn't be possible to evaluate whether the results were the same.

We are at the stage in compiling a dictionary of American gestures that Samuel Johnson was in compiling his dictionary of English words. Today preparers of dictionaries go through newspapers, books, magazines, internet communications, and recordings of radio and television to cull new words and verify their use. We have used television, and movies, and personal observations in our daily lives as sources for our list, but a more careful use of those and other sources is for the future. This is a beginning.

Gestures as equivalent to words or phrases
Compare the idea that a gesture (emblem) should have a verbal equivalent that is a word or short phrase to the same assumption for words, either within one language or in translation.

---

[18] Ekman, "Movements with Precise Meanings," 1976, p. 18. In that paper Ekman says:

> The methods have also been employed by three students who have worked with us: Harold Johnson in a study of middle-class, white, American males, Carol Turpin in her dissertation on Iranians, and Nitza Brodie in her master's thesis on Israeli students living in the United States for less than a year. p. 18

He gives no bibliographic references for these studies, and we have not been able to locate them.

Would a Brazilian say that a word or phrase in English isn't really a word or phrase if he couldn't translate it into a word or short phrase in Portuguese? There are words and phrases in English that resist any short definition even within English. We know what "for the sake of" means, but we cannot imagine any short definition of its meaning in other words in English, nor in Portuguese, Italian, or Spanish. That doesn't mean it's not possible to give such a definition, and I suspect someone could if he or she tried. But none comes naturally, and none would likely be considered equivalent by ordinary speakers. Yet we know perfectly well how to use that phrase, and to that extent we can say we understand its meaning.[19] How are gestures different? To restrict our attention to gestures that have short verbal equivalents is to narrow our subject too much, finding interest in gestures only to the extent that they can be substituted for pieces of language. To restrict our attention that way is to reject or at least ignore what is most different about gestures from verbal language.

Some words can be given a definition with a short phrase. Such a word can be thought of as an abbreviation, a shorthand for the phrase. But even that is not correct, for the word may have other values than simply being substitutable *salve veritate* that are different from the phrase. In any case, many words or semantically simple phrases do not have such definitions, even in terms of a com-plicated phrase. They have their meaning, and that is irreducible. To say that "dog" means "domestic canine" is to confuse what meaning is. At best "domestic canine" could be substituted *salve veritate* for "dog," but as a definition it is badly lacking because a fundamental criterion of a definition is that the words doing the defining are better understood than the word being defined.[20]

D. On the background of those collecting gestures

Without a clear description of how gestures are collected, and by whom, we do not have good reason to trust a gestuary to (i) include only gestures from that culture, (ii) be relatively complete, and (iii) include gestures that are common and not rare. Part of the description of any method of collecting gestures should be information about the background of those involved, particularly whether or not they are native speakers of the gestures.

This is why it is difficult to evaluate Saitz and Cervenka's collection: they do not tell us their background, most particularly whether they are American, or Colombian, or both. They give only a very brief description of the background of those they interviewed in the U.S. and no information about the background of their informants in Colombia.[21]

---

[19] *Webster's New World Dictionary of the American Language*, 1962, tries the shotgun approach to defining "sake":

> sake 1. motive; purpose; end; cause; : as for the *sake* of money. 2. advantage; behalf; benefit; account: as for my *sake*.

But "for *my* sake" just means "for the sake of me," and there is no difference in meaning of the phrase from its use in "for the sake of money." In any case, which is the definition? Pick and choose as appropriate by context? But that's just to say that there is no definition as a word or phrase that is equivalent. Yet the phrase "for the sake of" has a single meaning, it seems to us. If you say it doesn't, pointing to this definition, we would say that you are confused about meaning versus giving (rough) equivalents in other words.

[20] See Epstein, *Critical Thinking*, 2013, for criteria for a definition to be good. See Epstein, "Language-Thought-Meaning," 2015, for a further discussion of meaning.

[21] We have never seen the following American gestures from their collection: Disbelief (p. 42/I), Favor (p. 53/B), Insult (p. 78/E), and Leave (p. 81/E).

This is particularly important because, as with words, there is the problem whether a gesture is understood commonly or only by a particular group within the community, such as members of an ethnic group or workers in one occupation. For example, one day I noticed that my friend Walter Carnielli from Brazil made a gesture I didn't recognize as Brazilian or American, even though I had taught in Brazil and speak Brazilian Portuguese well. I asked Carnielli about it, who said it was Italian; Carnielli is third-generation Brazilian, his grandparents having immigrated from Italy. Another example: I read about a gesture in Colombia called *hacer la contraguiña* in which the hand is made into a fist palm inwards and the index finger and little finger are pointed downwards and touch a table, which is meant to ward off something bad or bad luck.[22] I wanted to know how to translate the Spanish. I asked a twenty-two-year-old Colombian student, Esperanza Buitrago-Díaz, who was working with me. She said she had never seen or heard of that gesture. I began to doubt the source from which I had learned the gesture, but then she asked some friends of hers in Colombia and found that it was a common gesture there. She didn't know it because she was raised in a religious home that eschewed superstitious gestures.

If all we know of the methodology of a gestuary is that the gestures listed are used by one or two informants from a country, we do not know if their responses, that is, the gestures they provided, are representative for that country or culture.

D. Our backgrounds

Here, then, are our backgrounds.

Richard L. Epstein is 67 years old and began compiling this list when he was 45. His parents were children of Jewish immigrants to the United States from Eastern Europe. He was raised in a small midwestern city, Des Moines, Iowa, and went to university in Philadelphia, London, and Berkeley. He taught logic and mathematics at universities in Iowa and Berkeley and taught at least one semester in Poland, in New Zealand, and in Brazil. He has written extensively on logic and critical thinking. He taught English as a second language in Berkeley and Cedar City, Utah, and lived for at least one month in Tahiti, France, Portugal, and Denmark. He speaks (or has spoken) American English, English English, New Zealand English, Polish, French, and Brazilian Portuguese, can read Italian and Spanish, and has a very limited knowledge of German. He is also a trained actor, director, and playwright. In the United States he has lived in Philadelphia (1965-1969), Berkeley/San Francisco (1969-1973, 1982-1989), Cedar City (a small town in Utah) (1989-1999), and, since 1999, in Socorro (a small town in New Mexico).

Alex Raffi is 45 years old and began working on this project when he was 30. His parents are immigrants to the U.S. from Paraguay; his grandparents are Italian. He was raised in Costa Mesa in southern California (1978–1990) though earlier he

---

[22] See the annotation of *American-Spanish Euphemisms* by Charles E. Kany, 1960, in the Annotated Bibliography below.

spent four years in Italy. Besides American English, he speaks Italian and Spanish.
He is a graphic artist and cartoonist who has illustrated a number of books and now
is the owner and artistic director of his own marketing and advertising firm. He is
married and has one daughter who is seven years old. He lives in Las Vegas,
Nevada, (1995–).

From 2002–2004 we discussed this project with Carolyn Kernberger, who
taught English as a second language in Albuquerque, New Mexico, in Micronesia,
and in Japan. She was born, raised, and went to university in New Mexico, and has
three children who at the time we were collaborating with her were ages 17, 22, and
26. Her family are from New Mexico.

All three of us are white and right-handed.

We showed our gestuary to many people who commented on the entries. But
over time we have lost track of their names.

III The Meaning of a Gesture

A. The message of a gesture

Compilers of collections of (classes like) conventional gestures accompany the presentation of each gesture with some verbal phrase or sentence(s).[23] There is no consistency about what such a verbal accompaniment is meant to be or do, even within a single compilation. For example, Johnson, Ekman, and Friesen in "Communicative Body Movements: American Emblems," 1975 give as the "message" or "verbal equivalent" of various gestures:

> "Whoopee" (accompanying words)
>
> "A close shave" (name of the gesture)
>
> "What time is it?" (a word or phrase that can be substituted)

In *Gesture, Race and Culture*, 1941/1972, David Efron presents a dictionary of Southern Italian conventional gestures used in New York. For making a circle around the eye with the thumb and index finger they have "Look out—You won't fool me—Derisive attention"; the first two are phrases that could be substituted for the gesture, and the third cannot. For extending the arm with the palm outward (like a school-crossing guard) they have "Command—Imperiousness—Stop—Salutation": only the third is a word that could either accompany the gesture or be substituted for it, while the last describes how it can be used. Some of their labels may be names of the gestures, but we are not familiar enough with those gestures to know.

Saitz and Cervenka, in *Handbook of Gestures: Colombia and the United States*, 1962/1972, describe their explanations:

> Descriptions of the gestures also include sample accompanying phrases when these seem particularly frequent or useful to the teacher or language student.
>
> In this edition, we also present tables of content in English and Spanish, an index which lists the semantic labels plus other content words from the descriptions which might aid a reader in locating the gesture.

Looking at examples from our gestuary, consider *High Five*. It is *called* "High 5"; if we were to ask someone to give us a High 5, we'd get that gesture. The *accompanying words* "All right!" are often spoken with it, especially when it's done in celebration in sports. If asked to give the *meaning* of the gesture, we might say it's a greeting, which describes *how it's used*, or in other contexts it is a way to

---

[23] However, David McNeill in *Hand and Mind*, 1992 says:

> Emblems are part of a social code but are not fully structured as a language. They have names or standard paraphrases, are learned as specific symbols, and can be used as if they were spoken words; in fact they are unspoken words (or phrases); but there is no grammar, and emblems are rarely if ever combined. p. 56

We note below in Section IV.A that some American conventional gestures are regularly combined.

express jubilation on account of an accomplishment, which is a description of the *emotion conveyed* by the gesture.

The message of a gesture is sometimes said to be its *verbal equivalent*. Sometimes there is a clear verbal equivalent in the sense of a word or phrase that could be substituted for the gesture, such as "Hi" or "Hello" for *Hello*. But some conventional gestures have no obvious verbal equivalent. For *Aw shucks–embarrassment* the phrase "Aw shucks" is often said with the gesture, but that is not the name of the gesture, nor a description of the movement of the gesture, nor the meaning of the gesture. We can say that the person is intending to show that he is pleasurably embarrassed, but that is a description of the emotion conveyed by the gesture, and it's not clear whether we should call that its meaning.

There are many other gestures that are accompanied by words, vocal sounds, or even whistles that are not part of a verbal equivalent. For *Nobody here but us chickens* an aimless, tuneless whistle is produced with the movement. The "verbal message" that is intended is not a word or short phrase, but something like "I'm acting as if I didn't do it, but of course we both know that I did, and I'm challenging you to say that I did."

Consider, too, *Nyahh, nyahh, nyahh–tongue out*. This is often called "Sticking your tongue out," which describes the movement but is not a name of the gesture. It's often, though not always, accompanied by the sounds "Nyahh, nyahh, nyahh" in the melody and rhythm noted there. Its "meaning" is a defiant challenge, which is a description of its use. It has no obvious verbal equivalent.

Some sounds that accompany gestures have become accepted as verbal equivalents because they elicit the image of the gesture, for example, *Whew!* and *Oops!* (imagine hearing them on radio). The first "means" that the person recognizes that he or she has just escaped a difficult or dangerous situation and is relieved. The second "means" that the person recognizes that he or she has just seriously bungled and wishes to let others know that. Recently American dictionaries have included such sounds, calling them "interjections"; their definitions show the same lack of clarity about what can be construed as the meaning of a word as we see with the meaning of a gesture.[24]

---

[24] From *Webster's New Twentieth Century Dictionary of the English Language, Unabridged,* 2nd edition, The World Publishing Company, 1968:

> *whew interj.* an exclamation of surprise, contempt, dismay, relief, etc.

"Oops" is not defined.

From *Random House Webster's Unabridged Dictionary*, 2nd edition, Random House, 2001:

> *whew interj.*   (a whistling exclamation or sound expressing astonishment, dismay, relief, etc.)
> *oops interj.*   (used to express mild dismay, chagrin, surprise, etc., as at one's own mistake, a clumsy act, or social blunder)

No explanation is given for why the entry is in parentheses. Note that on the usual understanding of what is a word, these are not words: they cannot be combined grammatically with other words in a sentence. If uncertain of the meaning, we cannot ask someone to use it in a phrase; we have to hear it

The meaning of other gestures is most clearly translated into English not by giving the accompanying sounds but by describing the movement or giving its name. For example, we often say "He gave a thumbs up" to convey the idea of approval even when the gesture *Thumbs up* has not been made.[25]

In summary, the phrases "the message of a gesture," "the verbal equivalent of a gesture," and more generally the verbal accompaniment of entries in compilations of conventional gestures have been used in quite different ways:

- A name of the gesture.

- A verbal equivalent.

- Words that accompany the gesture.

- A description of the gesture.

- The emotion conveyed by the gesture.

- A verbal definition of the meaning of the gesture.

- A description of how the gesture is used.

Not every conventional gesture has a word or phrase that could be substituted for it in conversation or communication. For some a sentence or two could be substituted. For others, only a description can be given of the reaction that is expected to be engendered in the person observing the gesture, or the emotion being expressed by the giver of the gesture, or how the gesture is used.

---

used in the context of some action, usually a gesture. Yet this dictionary defines:

> *interjection n.* 3. the utterance of a word or phrase expressive of emotion; the utterance of an exclamation. 4. *Gram.* a. Any member of a class of words expressing emotion, distinguished in most languages by their use in grammatical isolation, as *Hey! Oh! Ouch! Ugh!* b. any other word or expression so used, as *Good grief! Indeed!*

[25] Helmut Morsbach, "Aspects of Nonverbal Communication in Japan," 1973, notes a similar replacement of a gesture by a name of it in Japanese:

> Instead of saying outright that someone is suspected of being a liar, use can be made of the gesture called *meyutsuba* (eyebrow-saliva). Here, the index finger is briefly licked with one's tongue and then stroked over an eyebrow. (Originally it was a magical protection against being cheated by a fox.) According to Wgatsuma (personal communication), this has become old-fashioned. However, it is interesting to note that the gesture is now being verbalized. By uttering the word "*meyutsuba*" in the appropriate context, Japanese are able to imply dishonesty in someone without actually using the word liar. pp. 267–268.

María José Gelabert, Emma Martinell Gifre, TD-Guach, and Josep Coll Mestre in *Diccionario de Gestos con sus Giros Más Usuales*, 1990, give two examples of gestures in Spain whose meaning in Spanish is given by describing the gesture: (29) "Dos dedos" ("Two fingers") for a small quantity, and (64) "Mano sobre mano" ("Hand on top of hand") for inactivity. They also give (22), "Mas o menos" ("More or less"), a phrase that is likely to evoke the movement or the motor memory of the gesture to a Spanish speaker.

See also the comments by Kendon in "Abstraction in Gesture," 1992, p. 227 on the assumptions of the relation of gesture to verbal cliché in *The Semiotics of French Gestures* by Geneviève Calbris, 1990.

B. Gestures are complete utterances

Gestures are not like words. Only some, as described in Section IV, can be combined with others. Each is like a sentence or a complete utterance. Even some that are meant as assertions, such as *He's crazy*, have no obvious internal grammatical structure; only in translating them into English do we give them a noun-verb structure. Our gestuary is a bilingual dictionary from gestures into English.

David McNeill in *Hand and Mind*, 1992, says:

> Emblems are complete speech acts in themselves, but the speech acts they perform are restricted to a certain range of functions (Kendon, 1981[a]). They regulate and comment on the behavior of others, reveal one's own emotional states, make promises, swear oaths, etc. They are used to salute, command, request, reply to some challenge, insult, threaten, seek protection, express contempt or fear. In contrast to spontaneous gestures, however, they do not represent objects or events. Even when the iconicity of emblems is taken into account, the function is not referential or propositional. . . .
>
> Kendon raises the question why the social code of emblems is so restricted. Why are so few referential or propositional? p. 64

Speech act categories are meant to classify verbal utterances, not words or sentences. We can say the words "Ralph is a dog" in such a way that it is an assertion, a question, a warning, even a threat. If categories of speech acts are to apply to conventional gestures, then it must be to particular uses of those gestures.

We can't apply those categories by considering what verbal message the gesture is meant to convey, since, as we've seen, that is not only ambiguous but can be empty. Still, it seems that some gestures in their usual use are clearly meant as commands or requests, such as *Get up*, *Shhh*, and *Call me*. Others are clearly threats, such as *Staring– threat*, or are challenges, such as *Shaking your fist at someone*. Still others are queries, like *Time + Quizzical look*. Some are assertions, such as *Pointing* in many contexts. But many are difficult to classify. *Pat on the back* is usually used to express approval, but is that an assertion as when someone would say "You did a good job"? The usual use of *Pout* is in part an expression of an emotion and in part an assertion about the situation.

It might seem that we could test whether a conventional gesture is an assertion by asking whether it could be a lie. But we typically consider conventional gestures to be accurate reflections of the speaker's intent, like expressions of emotions, discounting the rare instances (we think) when they are produced to deceive. Thus, we take at face-value *Angry look*, *Aw, shucks–embarrassment*, *Blast!*, and many others and do not consider that they could be false. But does that mean that they are not assertions? If someone does *What a babe!* and you look and see a crippled old woman, you don't think the person is wrong; you assume that he is being sarcastic. If we are not clear about when to classify a conventional gesture as an assertion, then it's not clear that viewing gestures as speech acts will illuminate much.[26]

Adam Kendon in "Geography of Gesture," 1981, comments on the role of conventional gestures in communication:

> It will be noted that the range of meanings that emblematic gestures subserve is confined mainly to those that deal with the immediate interaction situation. Rather than being employed to convey statements about states of affairs beyond the immediate context, they address themselves for the most part to the problems of the interactive relationship or to the social situation. p. 142

This seems accurate for American conventional gestures as surveyed in our gestuary. But it seems less likely to be correct for those systems of gestures that allow for indications of time (see Section IV.F below), for to gesture of the past or future is not to gesture about the immediate interaction situation.

C. Meaning and context

To what extent is the meaning of a gesture determined by the context in which it is performed? And how much of that performance is part of the context?

Lorraine Kirk and Michael Burton, "Physical Versus Semantic Classification of Nonverbal Forms: A Cross-Cultural Experiment," 1976, say:

> According to Ekman and Friesen's definition, an emblem can be interchanged with an equivalent verbal form. We have chosen to leave as an empirical question to be investigated here the extent to which emblems are interchangeable with verbal forms of communication. Related to this is a second empirical question concerning whether emblems have meanings which are independent of the context in which they occur. Clearly, if the meaning of an emblem is heavily dependent on context, then it will be difficult to supply a word or phrase which can always replace it in speech. An example of extreme interchangeability would be a situation in which each emblem corresponded to one word or phrase, and in which the cognitive organization of the emblems was exactly the same as the cognitive organization of the corresponding lexical terms. At another extreme would be a situation in which the emblems did not have any mapping onto verbal forms in terms of meaning, and in which the meaning of an emblem varied idiosyncratically with the context of its use. pp. 459–460

Kirk and Burton must be using "emblem" to mean a symbolic movement that may have more than one meaning because an emblem, in the terminology established by Ekman and Friesen, always has a single verbal equivalent.

What is meant by "context" is rarely specified, nor are contexts usually specified in investigations of conventional gestures. Some researchers say it is unnecessary because they assume that each gesture they are investigating has a clear verbal equivalent. For example, Michaela Safadi and Carol Ann Valentine in "Emblematic Gestures among Hebrew Speakers in Israel," 1988, say:

---

[26] Gestures that are commands are truthful in the sense that normally the person can't both do them and not want the command obeyed; see, for example, *Come here*.

> "Emblems" will refer to gestures that convey specific messages, whose meanings are clear and unambiguous to the people who hold these acts in common even when they are performed out of context of conversation, and that are translatable into a word or phrase. p. 329

> Gestures here were tested out of the context of conversation. p. 358

But imagine saying the word "class" to a group of subjects and asking them to write down the meaning. Were we to deduce that the sound isn't a word because there isn't 90% agreement, we would be wrong or else using "word" in a very odd sense, for the meaning of that sound certainly depends on context in English.

Some researchers go further and exclude even facial expression from the performance of a gesture. They take a gesture to be determined solely by the movement of a very limited part of the body, requiring it to have an unambiguous meaning in all contexts.[27] For example, Safadi and Valentine say:

> During all tests, the investigator-encoder maintained a relatively neutral, unexpressive facial pose except where the affect [*sic*] of a smile versus a "neutral" facial expression was being checked. p. 349

But facial expressions are often crucial. For example, *The Finger* with an angry expression has a very different meaning from *The Finger* with a smile.

Pio Rico Ricci Bitti and Isabella Poggi in "Symbolic Nonverbal Behavior: Talking through Gestures," 1991, call facial expressions part of the context of a gesture:

> Gestures seem to be ambiguous much more seldom than words are, as there is always something in the nonmanual components of the gesture (trunk and shoulder posture, facial expression, etc.) or in the kind of movement by which the gesture is performed, that clarifies the gesture. . . . We might say that this is analogous to verbal language, in which the ambiguity of words is minimized by their context. p. 445

But then they note a different interpretation of the data:

> An opposing view could contend that nonmanual components are an intrinsic part of the gesture and not simply part of its context. According to this view, a gesture can never be ambiguous, simply because its nonmanual components convey a great amount of information. This leads to the conclusion that the lexicon of gestures is inherently different from a lexicon of words in that gestures are never really ambiguous. p. 446

Though the "non-manual" parts of gestures are often crucial in understanding what is meant to be conveyed, there do seem to be gestures that are identical movements with different meanings determined solely by the context in which they are used. For example, *Come here–head* and *Howdy–head* have exactly the same movement

---

[27] See, for example, Desmond Morris, Peter Collett, Peter Marsh, and Marie O'Shaughnessy, *Gestures: Their Origins and Distribution*, 1979, as discussed in the Annotated Bibliography below.

and facial expression; the movement of *Single nod yes* can be used to mean "yes" or as an acknowledgement, particularly of an introduction.

An example of the problem of not taking facial expression into account shows up in "The Brazilian Thumbs-Up Gesture," 1991, by Joel Sherzer. He investigates a gesture that we also describe as *Thumbs up*. He cites seven distinct usages, which he personally observed in São Paolo, Rio de Janiero, and Recife in Brazil, and he wishes to show all have a common meaning. All but one of them fit nicely into the description "positive," "good," or "OK." But the seventh does not:

> (7) As a request for permission to perform an action in a wide variety of situations.
>
> (a) A man wants to cross the street even though the light is against him. He makes the TUG [thumbs-up gesture] to a car moving toward him. The car stops for him, and he crosses the street.

To accommodate this usage, he has to come up with a more general conception of the meaning of the gesture having to do with social interactions. But it was obvious to us, and confirmed by our Brazilian colleague Walter Carnielli, that when the thumbs-up gesture is used in this way it is accompanied by the quizzical look, turning it into a question like "Is it OK?".

On the other hand, we have found that what we originally thought were different gestures could be understood better as one gesture with the same basic meaning used in different contexts. For example, we use the movement and facial expression of *Closer, closer* :

> When standing in front of an audience to request them to continue applauding, perhaps saying, "More, more."
>
> When someone is speaking slowly or hesitates in their speech to urge them to continue speaking, not using any words to accompany the gesture.
>
> When we want someone to approach us closer and/or more rapidly, perhaps saying "Closer, closer."

All of these can be understood as meaning "Continue what you're doing" or "Don't stop now." Judging by verbal equivalents, it seems, can be a very bad guide to what counts as the same or different gestures. This problem is exacerbated by the existence of many emphatics and diminutives, as we discuss in Section IV.D.

Some compilers of collections of gestures view the *context of a gesture* as we do: the actions and speech surrounding the performance of the gesture.[28] Some provide short dialogues or descriptions of a scenario; we use a cartoon to illustrate a context of use of a gesture.

---

[28] See the Annotated Bibliography for examples.

D. The difficulty of giving the meaning of a gesture

Morton Wiener, Shannon Devoe, Stuart Rubinow, and Jesse Geller in "Nonverbal Behavior and Nonverbal Communication," 1972, think that we should be able to give a dictionary of the parts of a system of communication:

> We have thus far in the paper loosely defined communication as the making public of experience with a shared code for encoding and decoding. The major concepts at issue in this definition are code and encoding, for only after these concepts are more fully explicated can the concepts of decoding and communication be understood within our perspective. We start with a definition of code which is essentially similar to a dictionary definition of code as a set of arbitrary components which have referents other than themselves. . . . *From this definition it follows that a dictionary of such elements and their referents could in principle be compiled.* Such a dictionary would be expected to change over time, however, in the same way that a dictionary of verbal forms changes. Further, while we could reasonably expect some behaviors to have more than one possible referent (as in verbal language some words have more than one referent), we assume that the number of referents for any given behavior would be finite and in principle specifiable, just as the several meanings of a given word are finite and specifiable. We further assume that the specific referent of a particular behavior in a particular context may be determined by its relationship to the rest of the communication matrix, again just as the meaning of a word in a given instance can almost always be specified on the basis of its relationship to other code components in the communication matrix. p. 203 [italics added]

It is not a consequence of the definition of "code" that a dictionary could be given. That assumes there is some way to designate the "referents" of the code other than by the code itself. It is not obvious that this is always possible. Part of the problem seems to be what these authors mean by "referent." On p. 210 they say, speaking of "pantomimic" gestures (roughly the idea of emblems), "such gestures have an object or event significance and function as nouns do in the verbal channel." If that is what they mean by "referent," they could say that the dictionary could be made by pointing—well, not actually pointing, but perhaps photos and videos. Another possibility, at least for American conventional gestures, might be to give the meaning of a gesture with a French or Brazilian conventional gesture. Or it might just be that we have no other way to state the meaning of *Aw, shucks*. We just know what it means. The assumption that a word, phrase, or sentence can be given for the meaning of a gesture seems to reflect a faith in verbal communication as the standard to which all other communication can be reduced.

Even for gestures that apparently have a verbal equivalent, such as *Hello*, the equivalence is doubtful. As Adam Kendon, "Geography of Gesture," 1981, says:

> It is said that gestures of this sort substitute for speech. This, however, is surely not really correct. It is true that these gestures are often used where speech could also be used, but it would seem that they are used by choice instead of speech

because the message they convey is *different* from the message that would be conveyed by any verbal expression by which they might be glossed. p. 138

And later in "Abstraction in Gesture," 1992, Kendon says:

> The impressively intricate ways in which gesture can serve to express meanings both concrete and abstract, displayed by Calbris [1990] with a richness no one else has matched, cannot be gainsaid. What are the implications?
>
> One implication is that of support for the view that the content that receives representation in utterance does not exist only in a language-like format; this, in turn, suggests that thought is, at least partially, imagistic in character. This position, though it has often been held (e.g., Arnheim, 1969), is by no means generally accepted, and the issue as to whether or not mental imagery and its manipulation are central and basic to thought, or whether they are phenomena derived from proposition-like descriptions, is yet to be settled. Bickerton (1990) has argued that thought is possible only if its elements are organized by (linguistic) syntax.[29]

The great difficulty of translating gestures into English suggests that English is not universal in the sense of a language capable of "expressing" any "thought."[30] We may not know how to find a verbal equivalent of a gesture such as *Aw, shucks*, but we know very well how to use it and respond to it; indeed, in trying to give the meaning of it we tend to repeat the physical movement. Meaning in this case is intimately tied to motor memory.

Our work apparently refutes the view that every thought is "organized by (linguistic) syntax." But that's only if what we mean by "language" is a verbal or sign language with full grammar. American conventional gestures have only a rudimentary grammar or syntax, as we discuss in Section IV, and so would not by themselves constitute a language. Perhaps, though, we should conceive of American English plus American gestures as one single language.[31]

E. Meanings and descriptions of gestures in our gestuary

The nature of meanings is elusive, and more so, it seems, for conventional gestures than for verbal or signed languages. In our entries we give what we hope is enough for a reader to discern some idea of the meaning of the gesture.

We first give each gesture a title. The title is the name of the gesture if there is one. If there is none, it is the word or phrase that is often spoken with the gesture and that would typically elicit an image of the gesture for most people, and we

---

[29] p. 245. The works he refers to are: R. Arnheim, *Visual Thinking*, University of California Press, and D. Bickerton, *Language and Species*, University of Chicago Press. See Epstein's "Language-Thought-Meaning," 2015, for more reasons to believe that thinking is not primarily linguistic.

[30] For further evidence of that, see Epstein, "The World as Process," 2015.

[31] Compare the title of Bruno Munari's 1963 gestuary for Italy: *Supplemento al Dizionario Italiano*. See also the quotation from Giovanni Meo-Zilio at the bottom of p. 94 below where he speaks of "gestures in the language of Uruguayans."

enclose that in quotation marks. If there is no such word or phrase, the title is a short description of the movement and/or meaning of the gesture.

After illustrating the gesture with a close-up drawing of the most important parts of the body involved, which we call a *headshot*, we note whether a phrase, or phrases, or sound can be spoken with the gesture. We then give the meaning, some idea of what the gesture is meant to convey. In some cases this is described as an emotion, in others, the reaction the gesture is meant to elicit. We often describe contexts in which the gesture can be used because often it is the context that makes the meaning clear. When there are two distinct meanings associated with a single movement or posture, we list two different gestures. This is comparable to treating "bark" meaning the sound a dog makes, "bark" meaning the outermost layer of a tree, and "barque" meaning a sailing ship as different words; they are *homonyms*, as are gestures that look the same but have different meanings. In some cases this results in our listing a metaphorical use of a gesture as a distinct gesture.[32]

---

[32] In contrast, many researchers take a gesture to be a symbolic movement regardless of what particular meaning it has. For example, Robert A. Barakat in "Gesture Systems," 1969, says:

> Meanings of these signs vary considerably from culture to culture. In fact, they vary considerably within a single culture, so that one gesture can have multiple meanings existing side by side at one time. p. 111

See also the discussion in the Annotated Bibliography below of Morris, Collett, Marsh, and O'Shaughnessy, *Gestures: Their Origins and Distribution*, 1979.

Compare the same issue for words, as described by John Lyons in *Introduction to Theoretical Linguistics*, 1971, pp. 405–406:

> How different must the meanings associated with a given form be before we decide that they are sufficiently different to justify the recognition of two, or more, different words? In their attempts to demonstrate the 'natural' origin of language, the Greeks introduced a number of principles to account for the extension of a word's range of meaning beyond its 'true', or 'original', meaning. The most important of these principles was *metaphor* ('transfer'), based on the 'natural' connexion between the primary referent and the secondary referent to which the word was applied. Examples of 'metaphorical' extension might be found in the application of such words as *mouth, eye, head, foot* and *leg* to rivers, needles, persons in authority, mountains and tables, respectively. In each instance there is discernible some similarity of shape or function between the referents. Various other types of 'extension' or 'transference' of meaning were recognized by the Greek grammarians, and have passed into traditional works on rhetoric, logic, and semantics. Meanings that are more or less clearly 'related' in accordance with such principles are not traditionally regarded as being sufficiently different to justify the recognition of distinct words. The traditional semanticist would not say that the *mouth* of a river and the *mouth* as a part of the body are homonyms; but rather that the word *mouth* has two related meanings. We have, therefore, in addition to synonymy and homonymy, what has come to be called in the more recent development of traditional semantics *multiple meaning* (sometimes called *polysemy*). The distinction between homonymy and multiple meanings is evident in the organization of the dictionaries we customarily use: what the lexicographer has classified as homonyms will be listed as different words, whereas multiple meanings will be given under one entry.

We follow the verbal description of the meaning of the gesture with one or more illustrations of the gesture used in context, what we call *context cartoons*, sometimes with a short commentary.

Perhaps from reflection on the entries in our gestuary it will be possible to come to a clearer idea of what is meant by or what we should mean by "the meaning of a gesture."

IV A Grammar of American Conventional Gestures?

American conventional gestures can be combined and modified in a number of regular ways.

A. Combinable gestures

Certain **combinable gestures** can be done simultaneously with many other gestures to add a specific meaning to the other gesture or to modify the meaning of the other gesture in a specific way. We note 9 of them in our gestuary, all of which involve principally the face and head:

> *Yes–nodding*
>
> *No–shaking the head*
>
> *Quizzical look*
>
> *Angry look*
>
> *Laughing*
>
> *Smile*
>
> *Biting your lip*
>
> *Intense look*
>
> *Irony–the long face*

Let's see how these can be used to modify the meaning of a gesture done simultaneously with it.

Consider *No–shaking the head*. By itself this indicates disagreement or disapproval. When done simultaneously with another gesture, it creates something like a negative of that one. But what does "something like a negative" mean?

> *You + No* This is pointing with your index finger at someone and shaking your head no. *You* by itself picks out someone; this gesture says it is not that person. In this case, adding *No* amounts to negating an assertion.

> *Money + No* The gesture *Money* is to rub your thumb and forefinger together in a circular motion, and it means that money is the subject of what is being paid attention to. Adding *No* does not mean that money is not the subject of discussion but rather is an assertion: "No money" or "I don't have money."

> *Time + No* To point with the index finger of your right hand to the top of your left wrist is a command: "Pay attention to the time" or "Be aware of the time." Adding *No* turns that command into an assertion: "There's no time" or "You're late."

> *Thumbs down + No* To give a *Thumbs down* is to express disapproval. To add *No* does not negate that disapproval but rather emphasizes it.

It is tempting to say that if a gesture is inherently negative like *Thumbs down*, adding *No–shaking the head* simply makes it more emphatic. But that raises the question what is meant by a gesture being inherently negative.

The *Quizzical look*, with head tilted forward and eyebrows raised, indicates questioning or doubt: "Are you sure?", "Is that right?", "Huh?". When added to another gesture that does not already have a set facial expression, or added after another gesture that does have one, it indicates doubt about what is meant by that other gesture or turns it into a question. For example, *Just a bit + Quizzical look* means "Are you sure you want just a bit?" or "Are you sure it was just a little bit?" depending on context. Doing the *Quizzical Look* simultaneously with *Time* means "What's the time?" or "Do we have time?" depending on context. This is very much like adding a question mark to the end of a sentence in written English or in spoken American English ending a sentence with a rising tone.

Irony–the long face indicates sarcastic disbelief. Doing *Irony* simultaneously with another gesture is like adding a sarcastic tone in spoken American English; the closest to a regular way of expressing that in written American English is to add "Oh, sure" to a sentence. For example, to do *Irony* simultaneously with *Just a bit* means what we might express by saying "Oh, sure, it was a little bit."

Many gestures can be modified to be a joke or not to be taken seriously, or literally by adding *Smile*, akin to the use of scare quotes in written language. For example, *The Finger* normally elicits and is meant to elicit strong negative feelings from the person to whom it's directed; but if two people are good friends and one of them says something disagreeable, perhaps jokingly, the other can respond with *The Finger* accompanied by a smile as a playful version of "Fuck you."

Some pairs of these combinable gestures can be combined, too, to give another combinable gesture with a meaning or role that is not simply the sum of its parts. For example, *Quizzical look + Yes–nodding* is the gesture *Please* which means what "Please" does in English. When this is done simultaneously with another gesture, it turns that one into a request. For example, *Just a bit + Please* means "Can I have just a little bit?" Interestingly, doing *No–shaking your head* with *Smile* gives *Bemused appreciation*, which has no negative significance at all: it indicates a bemused and slightly surprised appreciation.

These combinable gestures may be added to some gestures but not to all for which it would be physically possible. For example, we cannot add *Please* to *Handshake–acknowledgement*. We suspect that it will be difficult to give a clear explanation of the semantic roles of combinable gestures.

B. Pointing

In American conventional gestures, we point with a finger (*Finger point*), with our head (*Head point*), or with just our eyes (*Eyes point*). We point in order to draw someone's attention to some part of our experience. The movement indicates the direction to which we wish the other person's attention to be directed.

What do we point to? What do we wish someone's attention to be directed to?
We can point to pick out:

a person

an animal (a dog, a caterpillar)

a thing (a chair, a building, a tree)

a mass (mud, water)

an activity (running, eating)

a state of the weather (raining, sunny)

a place (near the doghouse)

a direction

We don't distinguish among these and other possibilities by any difference
in the movements, with two general exceptions. We have more specific kinds of
movements for people (*Me, You–singular, You-plural, Us, Them*)[33] and for
pointing in a direction or place behind us (*Pointing behind–finger*, *Pointing
behind–thumb*).[34]

All of us assume that pointing is unambiguous, completely clear. Indeed,
we feel it is the surest method of communication. It is so clear, we think, that we
confidently use it to teach someone our language: "dog" means that; "rain" means
that. But successfully communicating by pointing, conveying what part of our
experience we intend the other person to pay attention to, depends on a shared
background, shared experience, and shared purpose. Someone from a city who
has never been in a dense rain forest is unlikely to figure out what a native there is
pointing to among the mass of vegetation and life. Someone who hasn't been paying
attention to the sounds on a country path wouldn't likely understand when someone
points to the place where a bird song came from. Someone unconcerned with the
study of bugs is unlikely to discern what an entomologist is gleefully pointing to
on a dusty path.

But more profoundly, successfully communicating by pointing depends on a
shared language and more generally shared methods of communicating, including
our gestures. If I have a word for a particular kind of action, and you have none, it

---

[33] María Jose Gelabert, Emma Martinell Gifre, TD-Guach, and Jose Coll Mestre in *Diccionario de
Gestos con sus Giros Más Usuales*, 1990, describe such pointing as pronouns in their gestuary for
Spain, though they do not include pointing for "He," "She," or "They." Ana Maria Cesteros Mancera
in *Repertorio Básico de Signos No Verbales del Español*, 1996, also describes gestures for pronouns
in Spain.

[34] In contrast, John B. Haviland, "How to Point in Zinacantán," 2003, says that in the culture he
studied:

A distinction akin to that between linguistically marked genders or noun classes appears
to be conventionalized here in *symbolic* hand shapes that distinguish reference to
individuals from reference to pure direction. The flat hand apparently indicates "that
away" as opposed to the index finger's "that one." p. 160

might be fruitless for me to try to point to what is going on in order to draw your attention to it. If your language has no words for things but only process or happenings, it may be fruitless for me to point to a dog and have you understand that I mean that thing.[35]

Against our shared background and experience, relative to a context, we believe that we can make our meaning clear by pointing, perhaps not initially but by supplementing the pointing with more gestures, words, pantomime, or any other device we can think of to communicate better. For example, consider:

The man here might think that the woman is pointing to him (*You*). He gives the gesture *Moi?* (*Me + Quizzical look*) in return, and she shakes her head *No*. He then grabs his bowtie and straightens it, thinking she must be pointing to that. Again she shakes her head *No*. He gives the *Quizzical look* to indicate he doesn't understand. So she comes over to him and does the ultimate in pointing:

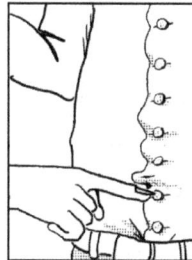

Even this might seem to be unclear: Does she mean to pick out the button or that he's

---

[35] See Epstein's "The World as Process" for process-talk versus thing-talk. See Epstein, *Predicate Logic*, 1994, for a fuller discussion of pointing used to pick out things relative to a given language.

buttoned his shirt incorrectly? Yet context, our paying attention to what is most unusual in our environment, will make it clear to the man that she means to draw his attention to his inept buttoning. If he's still uncertain, she can make her intention clear by rebuttoning his shirt correctly.

But now consider:

Is the pointing here meant to pick out the person ("That *man* there"), or the person sleeping ("He's sleeping"), or the snoring? The woman who is pointing might have had in mind just one of those as being most salient about the situation, but the gesture is nonetheless unambiguous: it picks out *that*—all of that situation. It is no more ambiguous than saying "See!" Just as with spoken and written language, we often mean to convey more. That we are unsuccessful is not a defect in the language; it's not a vagueness or ambiguity in the words or gesture.

This is not to deny that there can be vagueness or ambiguity. If someone says to his girlfriend that she should meet him at the bank near Second Street, she may be uncertain whether to show up at the financial institution there or at the river side. But everything we say is somewhat vague. Vagueness is inherent in our conventional gestures as in all our methods of communicating, though that does not mean our conventional gestures are too vague. Another example will illustrate this:

How should the girl interpret the pointing? Does the man mean the person who is planting flowers there? Perhaps the girl thinks he's pointing to the ground that's been turned up. Or does the man mean to pick out the planting of flowers there, or the ungainly posture of the woman? The girl looks puzzled, so the man adds the gesture for *He's crazy*:

Now it's clear that the man is pointing to the woman to show that he thinks she is crazy to be doing what she's doing. Still, it seems that the gesture is ambiguous among "She's crazy for planting flowers," "Lulabelle is crazy for planting flowers," "That woman is crazy for planting flowers," "The woman planting flowers is crazy," "The woman is crazy for doing that," . . . . But this ambiguity is in the translation of the gesture into English; the combination of gestures in this context is unambiguous.

Similarly for places: pointing is semantically indeterminate between the name of the place, a description of it, or a pronoun. But the indeterminacy is a verbal indeterminacy; there is no indeterminacy that we mean *this* place when we point— *if* the other person is attuned to seeing the gesture as meant to pick out a place.

This apparent ambiguity is a common phenomenon in translating from one language to another where the language being translated into demands more precision than the original language.[36] But, as the examples demonstrate, the indeterminacy of translation need not be an indeterminacy of meaning.[37]

Note that we cannot use American conventional gestures to refer to what is not present nor a place that is so distant that the direction to it cannot be well distinguished by pointing. For that kind of abstraction we need the supplement of words or pantomime.

C. Combining gestures sequentially

Pointing can be combined sequentially before or after another gesture. For example, we can do *Finger point* in the direction of somebody and then do *Poke in the ribs* as a command to note that person, or we can do those gestures in the reverse order to the same effect. We can do *Don't push me* and then point with a finger at something to show what it is that's making us angry.

Other gestures that are not generally combinable can be combined sequentially. For example, by first doing *That's that* (pretending to dust your hands) and then *Nothing–empty hands*, we have a combination that means there's no more, that's all there is. But generally, except for adding one of the combinable gestures or pointing,

---

[36] I was talking with a friend from Colombia, and I said, "My cousin is visiting tomorrow." We talked more about my cousin, and then my friend got frustrated and asked, "Is your cousin a man or a woman?" In Spanish the word "cousin" has to be marked for gender, so she considered what I said to be ambiguous.

[37] *Pace* Willard Van Orman Quine's analysis of "Gavagai" in *Word and Object*, 1960.

it seems that we don't combine gestures sequentially unless verbal communication is impossible. Each gesture is meant to be complete in itself, so a combination of them is just a sequence of complete utterances.[38]

D. Emphatics and diminutives

Adding certain of the combinable gestures to another gesture can make that other gesture more emphatic. For example, adding *Yes-nodding* to *Come here* is more emphatic than *Come here*. Adding *No–shaking the head* to *Stop!* makes the command more emphatic.

There are also standard ways in which we can modify a gesture to make it more *emphatic*:

- Do the gesture in a larger space with larger motion.
- Make the facial expression larger.
- Repeat the gesture.
- Use two hands rather than one.

The "opposites" of these modifications serve to make a gesture *diminutive*:

- Do the gesture in a smaller space with smaller motion.
- Make the facial expression smaller.
- Don't include a repetition.
- Use one hand rather than two.

For example, tilting the head down and then back to normal position just once is a diminutive of *Yes–nodding*. In contrast, repeating the nodding quickly in a larger motion, we get an emphatic.[39] By doing *Come here* in a very small space, we have a diminutive of it, while an emphatic is to do it with a broad sweeping motion. We can make an emphatic of *Stop!* by repeating it with a bigger facial expression or by using two hands instead of one.

---

[38] Fernando Poyatos in *Nonverbal Communication Across Disciplines*, 2002, p. 168, says (italics in the original):

> Emblems are used singly much more than in clusters, although *multiple emblems* are possible if, for instance, the verbal channel is occupied while we are on the telephone and signal to someone: "Hi/, /come in/, /sit down/, /read this/, I'll be with you in /two minutes/".

> There are also true *phrasal emblems*, as when a nod toward a poorly dressed stranger who walks into a reception and approaches the food table is followed by a shoulder shrug, a commiserative smile and a "stop" hand gesture, all together signifying "Oh, well, let him, poor fellow, he's hungry!", either alone or repeated by its verbal equivalent, sometimes this compound emblem being verbalized afterward.

[39] A number of authors have pointed out that repetition of a gesture, particularly nodding the head "Yes" or shaking the head "No," creates an emphatic form, e.g., Ambrosio Rabanales, "La somatolalia [Body language]," 1955, p. 368.

Other gestures have emphatics or diminutives that are peculiar to the gesture. For example, *Spitting*, which is meant to show disagreement or disapproval, has a range of versions from least to most emphatic:

- Moving your head to one side and expelling just a puff of air.
  This can be used jokingly with friends.

- Moving your head to one side and making a sound "P'tui" as if spitting out something that tastes bad.
  This can be used jokingly with friends.

- Moving your head to one side and actually spitting.
  This is very strong and not done except as an expression of serious contempt.

- Spitting at the other person.
  This is an expression of such serious contempt that it's an invitation to fight.

Still, even these could be seen as variations on the standard ways of making a gesture more or less emphatic. In contrast, adding a finger snap to *Come here* makes that more emphatic and is specific to just that and a few other gestures.

E. Gesture markers

Consider the following movements in which the arm is extended in front of the body, bent at the elbow, and the open hand is waved with:

Palm towards oneself.
    This means move (yourself or an object) towards me.

Palm away from oneself.
    This means move (yourself or an object) away from me.

Palm upwards.
    This means move (yourself or an object) upwards.

Palm downwards.
    This means move (yourself or an object) downwards.

Palm to the right.
    This means move (yourself or an object) to the right.

Palm to the left.
    This means move (yourself or an object) to the left.

Each of these can be viewed as a variation on a single gesture modified by the direction of movement. The marker is the ***direction***. We have no comparable marker in English.[40]

---

[40] In English we rely solely on context to indicate what direction we mean by "there." In Portuguese no grammatical markers are available for direction, but three different words are

We can also increase or decrease the speed of a gesture; by doing so we indicate how intense we want the action to be or how intent we are that the action be accomplished. This is an ***intensity marker***. When pointing to a place, we can indicate roughly how far it is from us by how far we extend our arm, which is a ***distance marker*** and is a kind of intensity marker, too.

In his study of Uruguayan gestures, "El Lenguaje de los Gestos en Uruguay," 1961, Giovanni Meo-Zilio, presents a system of what he calls *functional oppositions*, of which direction and intensity in American conventional gestures would be examples.[41] In "El Lenguaje de los Gestos en el Dominio Hispanófono: Comportamientos Morfosintácticos Y Derivacionale," 1986, he extends that work using comparisons across gesture systems of Latin America. These kinds of markers are similar to ones found in sign languages.[42]

F. A grammar of conventional gestures?

Andrea de Jorio was the first to point out that a system of conventional gestures could have a grammar. As Adam Kendon says:

> "Gestures," [de Jorio] says, "are not only adopted to express isolated ideas, but also ideas connected together" (317/293). This is done by coupling gestures together. De Jorio recognizes three different ways in which this can be done. First, gestures may be executed "one gesture after another, thus deliberately connecting one idea with the other". Second, two gestures may be executed in such a way that they are like two parts of a single action. Third, the meaning of a gesture can be altered by the circumstance in which it is performed, or sometimes by a modification of how it is performed, and in this way it may be used to express a combination of ideas.[43]

All these ways of modifying or combining gestures are available with American conventional gestures.

But the Neapolitan system of conventional gestures that de Jorio was studying also allows marking for tense:

> De Jorio explains that separate gestures are employed to indicate past (pointing behind oneself), present (pointing immediately downwards), and future (moving a laterally extended index finger forward in one or more arcs). These are added before or after the action referred to, as a way of indicating when it occurs in time. Likewise, de Jorio describes two gestures, either of which, he says, can be used to show that an action is being referred to in the abstract, that is to say, in the infinitive.[44]

used for location: aqui ("Here"), ali ("There where you are"), and lá ("There, distinct from where you and I are").

[41] See the list of those in the annotation of that article in the Annotated Bibliography below.

[42] For a popular exposition see Donna Jo Napoli, *Language Matters*, 2003, pp. 56–60.

[43] Introduction to de Jorio 1832/2000, p. lxxxvi. Some of the other collections of Italian or Neapolitan gestures discussed in the Annotated Bibliography below describe gestures for past, present, and future, but they do not discuss the use of them as tenses for other gestures.

Meo-Zilio in "El Lenguaje de los Gestos en el Dominio Hispanófono: Comportamientos Morfosintácticos Y Derivacionale," 1986, says that similar tense markers for gestures are used throughout Latin America. That and de Jorio's book are the only places we know where it is said explicitly that gestures for past, present, and future can act as tenses in conjunction with other gestures.

There are no American conventional gestures or gesture markers used to indicate relative times or time periods.

---

[44] Kendon, Introduction to de Jorio 1832/2000, p. lxxxiii.

V Some Classifications of Conventional Gestures

In this section we consider some ways to classify conventional gestures based on observations about American conventional gestures.

A. Homonyms, synonyms, antonyms

Gestures can be ***homonyms***: the same physical movement (with accompanying sound if that is the case) can have distinct meanings in different contexts. For example, the gestures *Come here–head* and *Howdy–head* are homonyms. A single nod down of the head can be used to mean "yes" or as an acknowledgement. Some apparent homonyms, however, are distinguished by their facial expressions. For example, an elbow in the ribs (*Poke in the ribs–joke*) has a smile, while an elbow in the ribs meaning "Shut up" (*Poke in the ribs–stop*) is accompanied by a grimace.

There are also ***synonyms***, gestures that can be used interchangeably. For example, *High Five*, *All right!–fist down*, and *All right!–fist up* are synonymous in any context where two people are celebrating.

Some gestures have what might be called an ***antonym***: a gesture that has the opposite meaning. But the idea of an antonym for a gesture is even less clear than an antonym of a word. We note such pairs only when it seems very obvious, as with *Yes–nodding* and *No–shaking the head* and with *Thumbs up* and *Thumbs down*.

B. Touch gestures

Touch gestures are conventional gestures that involve one person touching another. The gesture might be done by only one person with the other person a passive recipient of the touch, such as *Pat on the back–approval*. Or the gesture can involve two or more people actively, as in *Handshake–acknowledgement*.

C. Reciprocal gestures

Reciprocal gestures involve two or more people, whether one initiates it or they do it simultaneously and neither is passive. There are two kinds.

An ***active reciprocal gesture*** is one that requires two people to complete the gesture. Examples are *Handshake–acknowledgement* and *Hand slap–celebration*.

Responsive reciprocal gestures are done by one person and a standard response is expected. That may be a specific response as in *A toast!* Or it may be one of a range of responses as in *Nod of the head–acknowledgement*, where the other person can do any of the gestures of acknowledgement that are appropriate at a distance, such as *Nod of the head–acknowledgement* itself, or *Waving hello*, or *Howdy-finger*, or *Tip of the hat*, or even just *Smile*.

D. Refusals

If someone does not complete or respond to a reciprocal gesture, that in itself is a gesture, a ***refusal***. Depending on the kind of offer, context, and way in which the refusal is done, it can be mild or quite a strong rejection.

No thanks   Simply doing *No–shaking your head* indicates that you don't want to complete the gesture. This is polite. For example, you can refuse an offer of a piece of cake (*Offering an object*) this way.

Static refusal   You simply disregard the offer, doing nothing or continuing what you were doing. This is a gesture for which there is no specific movement. For example, you can refuse the offer of someone's hand in assistance (*Offering your hand in assistance*) this way. Depending on circumstances, this can simply indicate that you don't want what the other person is offering, or is impolite, amounting to ignoring the other person, indicating that he or she, or what they are offering, is of little concern or worth to you, as in *Refusing to shake hands*.

Active refusal   You look at the person or at the thing being offered and then look away, possibly with the expression *Supercilious/Contempt*. This is a definite rejection.

Strong rejection refusal   You look at the person or at the thing being offered and then do *Get out of here–palm* or *Turning your back on someone*. This is an emphatic expression of contempt or disgust.

E. Sarcastic gestures

We have found only a few American conventional gestures that are invariably sarcastic. We indicate sarcasm more often by adding *Irony–the long face* to a gesture. Context can also determine a gesture to be sarcastic, for example, *Scoring a point* used when the other person has done something stupid. Much depends on the facial expression.

F. Status-restricted gestures

Some gestures are normally done only to an equal. For example, *You're hot* done to a superior would be a major breach of status and very impolite, while done to an inferior would be rude and cruel. Others can normally be done to an equal or inferior but not to a superior, such as *Irony–the long face*, or *Angry look*, or *You–singular*. Still others are done principally to a superior or someone with whom the gesturer is not acquainted but not to an obvious inferior, for example, *Bowing* and *Standing on being introduced*. When these gestures are done across status boundaries, they have not only their usual meaning but a significance of a conscious breaching of status and, with that, rudeness, cruelty, or challenge.

G. Gender-restricted gestures

Some gestures are restricted by gender. They are done by only:

   a man to a man   (*Glad-handing*)

   a man to a woman   (*Kiss a woman's hand*)

a man to either a man or a woman   (*Tip of the hat*)

a woman to a man   (*Batting your eyelashes*)

a woman to either a man or a woman   (*Curtseying*)

a woman and a man   (*Kiss on the mouth*)

a woman and a man or a woman and a woman   (*Walking arm-in-arm*)

We have found no American conventional gesture that is done only by a woman to a woman.[45] Indeed, the only example of a gesture done only by a woman to only a man beside *Batting your eyelashes*, which is nearly archaic now, is *Exposing your breasts*, which is at best marginally classified as a gesture rather than simple exhibitionism.

These classifications, which we index in the gestuary, are often difficult to determine since many gestures that were previously done only by men are now used by women (and therein lies a story). For example, fifty years ago it was unimaginable for any but the most coarse woman to do *The Finger*, though it is not uncommon now. Also, gestures that we list as man to woman or woman to man might be done by pairs of homosexuals, for it is gender not sex that is determinant. The comments of Stephenson, Pine, Liwei, and Jian on gender restrictions of Chinese gestures in "Some Gestures Commonly Used in Nanjing, PRC," 1993, apply to American conventional gestures, too:

> Gesture use is also influenced by gender; some gestures exist in male and female forms that are similar, but readily identifiable as being appropriate to one sex but not the other. For example, informants identified waving to someone at a distance with the arm extended as male, and the same gesture with the hand held close to the body as female. Members of both sexes may feel silly when making the opposite-sex form of the gesture, and the appearance is frequently ludicrous. At one time obscene gestures were considered male prerogatives, but this is changing, at least among American women, as freeway drivers and rush-hour motorists can attest.   pp. 237–238

A further issue is to what extent gender influences the amount or style of gesturing. The only study we know that addresses the relative amount of use of gestures by men versus women is by Tommy H. Poling, "Sex Differences, Dominance, and Physical Attractiveness in the Use of Nonverbal Emblems," 1978, who reports:

> An examination of the interaction of subjects' sex [versus] subjects' attractiveness indicates that highly attractive women use emblems with greater frequency than

---

[45] Compare Laurence Wylie, *Beaux Gestes: A Guide to French Body Talk*, 1977, which despite it's title is a compilation of conventional gestures:

> For a people reputed to be absorbed with sex, there is a very short list of gestures related to it, and even these are not very sexy. They are also all gestures made by men, since the French women in our research group looked for gestures women might make and found none.

do women of low attractiveness or men of either high or low attractiveness. Emblem use did not differ as a function of attractiveness for men.

H. Sexual and obscene gestures

Some gestures are *sexual* but not obscene. For example, *Limp wrist* is meant to indicate that the person referred to is a homosexual. Indeed, whether a gesture such as *She's stacked* is obscene rather than just rude is very much in the eye of the beholder. Some gestures, though, are universally considered *obscene*, such as *Wiggling your tongue* or *Eat me!*.[46] Some of those are comments, some are sexual invitations, and some are challenges.

I. Obscene humiliations

We sometimes talk of one person pissing on another, meaning doing something bad, degrading, or demeaning to the other person. It is figurative talk, but it comes from the image of one person actually pissing on another. To do that would be the maximal expression of contempt and domination by the person doing the pissing. But would it be a gesture?

How do we distinguish pissing on someone from what we've seen in movies where one person pushes someone's head into a toilet bowl? That, too, is a sign of dominance and contempt. Neither is done often in our society; indeed, most people would never see either in their lifetime. Yet all of us would recognize them for what they are.

The difference, we think, is that the latter isn't a sign of dominance and contempt—it is the actual dominance and contempt. Pissing on someone expresses the dominance and contempt, being as much symbolic as literal, which is why a description of it has come into our spoken language. It is as symbolic as spitting, which is unquestionably a conventional gesture. Still, "shitting on someone" has also entered our language, yet we would not consider the actual action to be symbolic because we can't imagine anyone doing it. These distinctions are hard to make, so we have not attempted to include as gestures actions whose sole meaning is an obscene expression of domination and contempt.

J. Iconic gestures

Some researchers pick out a subclass of (a class like) conventional gestures as being iconic. For example, Ekman and Friesen in "The Repertoire of Nonverbal Behavior: Categories, Origins, Usage, and Coding", 1969 say,

> Acts which are intrinsically coded carry the clue to their decoding in their appearance; the nonverbal act, the sign, looks in some way like what it means, its significant. p. 60

---

[46] According to Saitz and Cervenka, *Handbook of Gestures: Colombia and the United States*, 1962/1972, there are many more obscene gestures in Colombia.

They consider the example:

> The tracing of the body outline of a woman is an iconic-pictorial emblem
> in which the hands draw a picture of a shapely woman to state sexual
> attractiveness. p. 65

This is our *What a babe!*, but it is not iconic in their sense. The figure described
by the gesture looks somewhat like the figure of the woman it refers to, but what the
gesture means, its "significant," is not the woman, nor her shape, but, as Ekman and
Friesen note, that she has a good shape and is sexually attractive.

Another example Ekman and Friesen give of an iconic gesture is also not iconic
by their definition:

> If a person runs a finger under his throat to signify 'having one's throat cut' or
> more figuratively, 'an unfortunate outcome', this is iconic coding since one cannot
> cut a person's throat with the finger, and the finger is standing for the knife. p. 61

Cutting one's throat does not look like an unfortunate outcome, for example, failing
a test. It is, as Ekman and Friesen say, figurative, and hence an arbitrary symbol.
Making barking noises to imitate a dog is iconic; making barking noises to suggest
that a person has nothing to say is not iconic. William Washabaugh, "The Manu-
Facturing of a Language," 1980, says,

> So-called iconic signs, such as those mentioned above, should not be called
> "naturally representative of their referents". In these examples, there is not so
> much a relationship between the sign and the referent, as between the sign and
> the culturally conventionalized image of the referent.[47]

In his Uruguayan gestuary, Meo-Zilio describes a class of gestures like our
conventional ones and then defines a notion of *icastic* gesture:

> The *representative* [gestures], in turn, can be classified as:
>
> a) *representative-symbolic*, more abstract, more arbitrary (more *linguistic*);
>
> b) *representative-icastic*, allusive or imitative of concrete situations, mood
> (abstract?) or quite material. These last can go from a remote reference, indirect
> with relation to the implicated concrete situation, to an immediate reference,
> direct, merely reproductive ; in sum, they can have a certain degree of abstraction,
> but not *symbol*, that is, conventional and arbitrary *sign* as, on the other hand, the
> representative-symbolic ones.[48]

---

[47] p. 3. This is the best discussion we have found on the nature of iconicity in gestures and signing.
[48] Meo-Zilio, 1961a, p. 91:

> Los *representativos,* a su vez, pueden clasifarse en:
> a) *representativo-simbólicos*, más abstractos, más arbitrarios (más *linguisticos*);
> b) *representativo-icásticos,* alusivos o imitativos de situaciones concretas, animicas, o
> bien materiales. Estos últimos pueden ir desde una referencia lejana, indirecta con
> relación a la situación concreta implicada (*alusión*), hasta una referencia immediata,
> directa, meramente reproductiva (*imitación*); en suma, puede hablar en ellos cierto

Efron, in his analysis of body language, speech markets, and conventional gestures, 1941/1972, defines a class of gestures he considers iconic. But in a footnote to that passage, he recognizes the difficulty in describing gestures that way:

> Needless to say, the difference between the pictorially and the non-pictorially symbolic movements is purely formal. Referentially they are identical, for the pictorialism of the former has nothing to do with the pictorial qualities of the object it represents. There exist, however, certain cases in which the symbolic gesture possesses a partial descriptive relationship to the thing represented. These "hybrid" (referentially speaking) movements are hard to classify, for they fall under two categories. p. 96

What is iconic is relative to a culture. Consider the movements of a hand held in front of the body at shoulder height with the palm out and pushed away and the same posture with the palm towards yourself and moved toward yourself. We consider each of these iconic: the direction of movement and palm corresponds exactly with the direction of movement we want to convey to the other person, so the first means "Go away" and the second means "Come towards me." But in Italy those movements have exactly the opposite meaning.[49] Our experience adjusts how we see the world, so that the gesture *What a babe!* looks just like a sexy woman's outline—to us. And *Sleep* looks just like a person sleeping—to us. Perhaps people from another culture would see those similarities; perhaps not. What is iconic is in the eye of the community of beholders.

The difficulty, which is not unique to gestures, is to give a clear explication of the idea that a symbol "looks like" a thing or an action. It seem that what is iconic is established conventionally, but once established, perhaps on the basis of some resemblance that first only one person but then many of us in our culture recognize, it is viewed as representative in some manner that is not purely symbolic.[50]

---

grado de abstracción, pero nunca *símbolo*, este es, *signo* convencional y arbitrario como, en cambio, sucede en los representativo-simbólicos.

[49] See Jay Leone, *Italian without Words*, 1992, pp. 84–83 and pp. 88–89.

[50] This is similar to the view of Sherman Wilcox in "Cognitive Iconicity: Conceptual Spaces, Meaning, and Gesture In Signed Languages," 2004, which surveys definitions of iconicity. The entire issue of the journal in which that appears is of interest for relating signed languages and gestures. See also Kendon, 1981b, pp. 34–36, for a discussion of the difficulty in classifying gestures as iconic. See also Catherine Z. Elgin, "Index and Icon Revisited," 1996, who says, "Something is an icon or index only if it functions as such," p. 183 Meike Adam, Wiebke Iversen, Erin Wilkinson, and Jill P. Morford, "Meaning on the One Hand and on the Other," 2007, show within a general discussion of iconicity that what is considered iconic in a sign language is not independent of the particular sign language and culture.

VI Are There Universal Conventional Gestures?

Weston LaBarre in "The Cultural Basis of Emotions and Gestures," 1947, scotches the most likely candidates for universal gestures: in some cultures "Yes" or "No" is not done by nodding or shaking the head; pointing with the index finger of an extended hand to draw attention to an object is not universally used nor recognized.[51] Mary Key, "Gestures and Responses: A Preliminary Study among some Indian Tribes of Bolivia," 1962, annotated below, contains material that makes the possibility of any universal gesture seem remote.

Safadi and Valentine, however, disagree. In "Emblematic Gestures among Hebrew Speakers in Israel," 1988, they say,

> Another universal behavior seems to be the smile. . . . Smiling in advance of other nonverbal or verbal behavior seems universally human. p. 343

> The postulate, that the smile is a universal gesture of happiness, is supported by virtually all the literature on facial expressions. p. 344

But they themselves show that this is wrong:

> Though a smile is essentially an indicator of happiness, its additional connotations and functions can vary. Among Puerto Ricans, a smile can replace a verbal politeness formula [reference]. Smiling is a social duty in Japan to avoid inflicting negative feelings on others [reference]. A smile is an indication of attractiveness in the United States, especially for women [reference]. A smile can also be an aspect of appeasement behavior, particularly in children and women [reference]. The problem that arises is to correctly assess the internal state of a smiling person one must understand how that gesturer was taught to manipulate that behavior for social purposes. p. 344 [52]

---

[51] Roman Jakobson, "Motor Signs for 'Yes' and 'No,' " 1972, surveys various ways of gesturing "Yes" and "No," and Joel Sherzer, "Verbal and Non-Verbal Deixis: The Pointed Lip Gesture among the San Blas Cuna," 1972, describes pointing with the head and face among the San Blas Cuna.

I. Eibl-Eibesfeldt in "Similarities and Differences between Cultures in Expressive Movements," 1972, suggests that the "eyebrow flash" (like our *Howdy–head*) may be universal, but then says on p. 10, "We are normally not aware that we use this signal, but we respond strongly to it in greeting situations." He discusses other candidates for gestures that may be universal, particularly shaking the head no, citing approvingly evolutionary explanations for that. Adam Kendon, "Did Gesture Have the Happiness to Escape the Curse at the Confusion of Babel?", 1984, says that pointing is universally understood, which is weaker than saying that it is a universal gesture. But David Wilkins in "Why Pointing with the Index Finger Is Not a Universal (in Sociocultural and Semiotic Terms)," 2003, reports on a communication from Mike Olson that the Barai of Papua New Guinea do not use or understand index-finger pointing.

[52] Morsbach in "Aspects of Nonverbal Communication in Japan," 1973, says that in Japan a smile in a conversation should be understood as a nervous grin, an indication that the person is very uncomfortable and wishes you would change the subject. As Jack Seward, *Japanese in Action*, 1968, says,

> The Japanese, like us, smile when they are pleased, when they are happy, and when they see something that amuses them. But they also smile when they are embarrassed and

Part of the difficulty in evaluating a claim that a gesture is universal is that it's not clear whether someone is talking about a particular movement that is symbolic or the movement plus its meaning. The same movement may be used for quite different meanings in different cultures, and it hardly seems accurate to say that the same gesture is used in those cultures.[53]

We said in Section I.B.6 (p. 8) that a sufficient condition for a nonverbal act to be symbolic is that someone from at least one other culture cannot understand it without explanation. If there are no universal gestures, then that is also a necessary condition for an act to be symbolic. Wiener, Devoe, Rubinow, and Geller in "Nonverbal Behavior and Nonverbal Communication," 1972, suggest that this is indeed correct:

> To find invariance of behavioral form and referent across cultures would to us be prima facie evidence that the behavior is not part of a coding system. We could agree that some forms of behavior (e.g., facial variations) might be more likely than others to be used in making public some sets of experience (e.g., mood state). However, a behavior whose significance is found to be invariant across cultures (i.e., observers attribute the same significance to the behavior in all cultures) would be difficult to include as a code component, which for us involves an assumption of an arbitrary relationship between symbol and referent. Rather, we would subsume such behaviors under the rubric of stimulus-specific behavior sequences—even if the behaviors occur under different conditions in different cultures [references]. p. 203

We agree. Still, a gesture could be adopted by transmission from culture to culture and eventually become universal. Perhaps a candidate might be *Surrender* where the hands are held above the head, though we wouldn't bet our lives on it.

---

when they are sad and wish to shield others from their sadness. And when they are perplexed and when they are angry. p. 132

[53] This is the point that Wilkins makes in "Why Pointing with the Index Finger Is Not a Universal (in Sociocultural and Semiotic Terms)," 2003. Yet such identifications are made by Morris, Collett, Marsh, and O'Shaugnessy, in *Gestures: Their Origin and Distribution*,1979, as discussed in the Annotated Bibliography below.

VII The Evolution of Gestures

David McNeill says of the history of gestures:

> Nonconventional gestures have zero depth. They are ephemeral creations by
> individual speakers. Conventional gestures, by contrast, have existed in more
> or less the same form for centuries or millennia.[54]

But an unstandardized gesture used by one person may have been produced by many
people over many centuries: we have no reason to think that we are the first to
describe a box by roughly setting out its shape with our hands. What distinguishes
an unstandardized gesture from a conventional gesture is not its being ephemeral, but
that its form is not recognized as a standard: it is not part of the language of gestures.

McNeill also claims:

> While no spoken languages have lasted unchanged since Roman times, a number
> of emblem gestures are Roman and some are older than that.[55]

But a conventional gesture is more similar to a single word or phrase than a
language, and some words and phrases have persisted unchanged since Roman
times.[56]

Though some gestures may have persisted over millennia, others are created
and fall out of use much like slang. Some of the many American gestures that are
common now but, we believe, were unknown seventy-five years ago are *High Five*
and *Got'cha*. A very recent one is *Loser*.

In contrast, we call a conventional gesture **archaic** if it was once common but
now is unknown or extremely rare. An American gesture that has become archaic in
our lifetime is the *mano cornuta* or "Horns," which is done with the hand about
chest level, back of the hand facing outward, and only the index finger and little
finger raised. This used to be an obscene challenge in the United States, but it now
holds no meaning for most of the population or else might be confused with a gesture
of support for the University of Texas athletic teams ("Hook 'em horns").[57]

---

[54] McNeill, "Speech and Gesture Communication," 1998, p. 15.

[55] McNeill, *Hand and Mind*, 1992, p. 60.

[56] McNeill suggests that gestures persist unchanged because a gesture cannot be varied even
slightly and still be understood as the same gesture. That might be true for the single gesture he
considers, *A-OK*, but that one example is not sufficient to establish his generalization.

[57] The gesture dictionary of Saitz and Cervenka compiled in 1962 shows several American gestures
we have never seen, particularly 42 I, 43 top and bottom, 53 B, 78 E, 81E, 95, 99 top, 102 E, 109 F,
110 H, 110 I, 140 D.

Levette Davidson, " Some Current Folk Gestures and Sign Language," 1950, p. 4, lists two
gestures we assume she considers common in the U.S. that we do not recognize as American:
"Placing fingers on head to represent horns is one way of calling a person 'cuckold'; to make 'a fig,'
by thrusting the thumb between the first and second finger, is an obscenity, indicating that you don't
give a fig for the one who has incurred your displeasure."

An example of how the meaning of a gesture can evolve over time is that of raising the index and middle fingers in the shape of a "V" palm outward in front of the body (see *Peace*). During World War II this came to mean "Victory." In the late 1960s the next generation took it to mean "Peace." The present generation often understands it as a friendly greeting. Three succeeding generations gave the same physical movement three successive, distinct meanings.

What American gestures have become archaic in the last fifty years? One hundred years? Is there a pattern to the kind of gestures that have become archaic? These are urgent questions because in order to answer them we should interview the elderly before the experience of now-archaic gestures is lost.[58]

---

[58] Efron, 1941/1972, pp. 123–124 cites references and on pp. 153–154 some research he did that may make possible such a study for Southern Italian gestures in relation to his dictionary of those gestures in 1941 (pp. 201–216), both in comparison to now and those current in 1832 as described by de Jorio, 1832/2000.

Jean-Claude Schmitt in "The Rationale of Gestures in the West: Third to Thirteenth Centuries," 1991, discusses the difficulty of using printed sources and art work to infer the movements and use of gestures from times for which we have no other records.

VIII   Describing and Organizing Gestures in a Gestuary

How we understand and investigate conventional gestures depends in part on how they are presented to us in collections of gestures.

A. Describing gestures

Four main ways have been used to describe or illustrate collections of gestures.

1. Verbal descriptions

Many collections of gestures describe all (but a few) gestures only in words.[59] This has the advantage of isolating the movements involved, though rarely are the accompanying facial expressions carefully noted. Cláudio Basto, "A Linguagem dos Gestos em Portugal," 1938 comments on the limitation of this method in his gestuary for Portugal:

> The descriptions will be brief, schematic. The *gestures*, which I single out, are accompanied, as a rule, by other body postures, especially facial expressions,— and the minute description of the mutual ensemble of physical movements, for each *gesture*, would make this too long, tedious,—and not useful. The description would always be far from perfect; one could not, in the end, give an exact representation, the lifelike image of the whole mime, to someone who has never observed it carefully.[60]

This does not seem different from a dictionary of words. We cannot give the exact pronunciation of every word, nor the exact context of use of each. We have stylized pronunciation guides, but still it is hard for someone who has never heard the phrase "Got you" said aloud in American English to learn from a dictionary how it is pronounced ("Gotcha"). A gestuary, just like a dictionary, is a guide to someone learning the language. It is difficult if not impossible to learn to understand and use a language without exposure to its use (speaking, gesturing).

In describing gestures only verbally there is a further problem: the descriptions do not provide a ready reference to the gestures that can be recognized at a glance, which seems essential in doing research.

2. Photographs

Many collections of gestures illustrate each with one or more photographs.[61] This

---

[59] For example, as described in the Annotated Bibliography below, Giovanni Meo-Zilio, *El lenguaje de los Gestos en el Río de la Plata,* 1961; Betty J. and Franz H. Baüml, *A Dictionary of Gestures,* 1975; Chet A. Creider, "Towards a Description of East African Gestures," 1977.

[60] As descrições serão breves, esquemáticas. Os *gestos*, que individualizo, acompanham-se, em regra, de outras posturas corporais, especialmente de expressăso fisionómica,—e a descrição minuciosa dos conjuntos solidários de movimentos físicos, para cada *gesto*, tornar-se-ia demasiado longa, fastidiosa,—e inútil. A descrição ficaria sempre longe de perfeita; não conseguiria, ao final, dar a representação exacta, a imagem viva dos conjuntos mímicos, a quem nunca os tivesse bem observado. p. 5

[61] For example, as described in the Annotated Bibliography below, R. A. Barakat, "Arabic

has the advantage that the illustrations can be included in the text, and it is relatively inexpensive to take and reproduce photographs of people. It is difficult, though, to indicate movement in photographs; some authors use arrows drawn on the photos, other use sequences of photos or stopgap photography. The real problem, though, is that it is difficult to judge what is significant and what is idiosyncratic to the particular person(s) in the photo. We judge the entire scene, and much that is extraneous often seems important as our eye is drawn to the particular rather than the schematic. Laurence Wylie, *Beaux Gestes*: *A Guide to French Body Talk*, 1977, has done good work in overcoming these problems: he uses a single person who is a trained actor, himself, dressed in a black turtleneck sweater to isolate exactly what is important in the movement. However, his approach isolates the movement from the context of the gesture; making photographs of contexts of gestures will be more complicated and expensive and introduce even more extraneous elements.

3. Films and video
Some use films of people gesturing. Efron in *Gesture, Race and Culture*, 1941/1972, describes the use he made of film in analyzing speech markers, but apparently he did not use film for recording conventional gestures. Efron's films were not made available to others, and we do not know if they still exist. Johnson, Ekman, and Friesen "Communicative Body Movements: American Emblems," 1975, describe how they used videos to verify emblems, but apparently never made those available to others. Calbris in *The Semiotics of French Gestures,* 1990, says that she made films, but apparently did not make those available to the public. David Wylie and Alfred Guzzetti filmed French gestures, but that work is available only at the Harvard Film Archive. Joseph Chandler Walz, "Filming French Gestures," 1979 (annotated below) discusses the process of making a film of French gestures, though his film, too, is not available.

Using the Internet it is now easy to make available video illustrations of gestures, as Emma Martinell Gifre and Hiroto Ueda do in *Diccionario de Gestos Españoles*, 2002. But, as discussed in the annotation to that work below, determining what is significant and what is idiosyncratic to the particular person making a gesture is very hard with videos.

4. Sketches
A number of gestuaries, including ours, use sketches to illustrate the movement of a gesture.[62] These have the advantage that particular motions can be isolated in the

Gestures," 1975; Don Cangelosi and Joseph Delli Carpini, *Italian without Words*, 1989; Phyllis Harrison, *Behaving Brazilian*, 1983; Barbara Monahan, *A Dictionary of Russian Gesture*, 1983; Monica Rector and Aluzio R. Trinta, *Comunicação Não-Verbal: A Gestualidade Brasileira*, 1986; Guido Indij, *Sin Palabras/Speechless*, 2006; and Hamiru•aqui, *70 Japanese Gestures*.
[62] For example, as described in the Annotated Bibliography below, Efron and Van Veen, 1941/ 1972; Martin Meissner, Stuart B. Philpott, and Diana Philpott, "A Dictionary of Sawmill Workers'

picture, and facial expressions can be clearly noted in a schematic way, drawing attention to only what is essential in the movements. Some illustrators have also devised ways to indicate motion.[63] Further, a reader can readily recognize and compare gestures when surveying the gestuary.

The drawback of this method is the difficulty of finding a competent illustrator who must become an equal partner in compiling the gestuary.[64]

5. Contexts

One problem common to all gestuaries is how to describe contexts in which a gesture can be used. For dictionaries of spoken languages, it is common to indicate only whether a word is obscene, rare, or vulgar, leaving the reader to discern more through experience. However, for gestures it is often crucial to note the relative positions of more than one person in the performance of a gesture, what the people are doing, gender restrictions on its use, and whether the gesture is meant to be performed only to a superior or inferior. Context can radically change the meaning of a movement, as we have discussed above. Most gestuaries include at least some comments about the appropriate use of gestures.[65] In our gestuary we have partly addressed this problem by using context cartoons to illustrate at least one archetypal use of each gesture, with accompanying commentary. We believe that this method, including indications of movement in the pictures, where the illustrations are shown to non-speakers of the gesture language to verify that someone can reproduce the gesture from the illustrations, is the best for printed materials. And we believe that for ready reference in doing research, printed materials are essential, though we expect that supplements of motion cartoons and videos which include sounds that are typically made with the gestures will be standard in the future to the extent that funding allows.

Another problem in illustrating gestures is how to show whether it is important that the right hand or left hand is used since people tend to imitate by mirror image. This is compounded by needing to note whether it is indeed the right hand that is used or rather the dominant one. We simply add a comment to the drawing.

Signs,"1975; Robert L. Saitz and Edward Cervenka, *Handbook of Gestures: Colombia and the United States,* 1962/1972; and Carol Magda Pearson Sparhawk, *Linguistics and Gesture: An Application of Linguistic Theory to the Study Of Persian Emblems,*1976.

[63] A notably clear method of illustrating motion in drawings of gestures can be found in Garrick Mallery, *Sign Language among North American Indians Compared with that Among Other Peoples and Deaf Mutes*, 1880, pp. 550–552.

[64] Fernando Poyatos, "Gesture Inventories: Fieldwork Methodology and Problems," 1975, pp. 384–385, says that film is superior to still photographs, which he considers superior to cartoon illustrations.

[65] For example, María José Gelabert, Emma Martinell Gifre, TD-Guach and Josep Coll Mestre, *Diccionario de Gestos con sus Giros Más Usuales,* 1990, present written dialogues, while Gifre and Hiroto Ueda, *A Gesture Inventory for the Teaching of Spanish,* 2002, illustrate contexts of gestures in video dialogues.

B. Arranging entries in a gestuary

A great difficulty in creating a gestuary is deciding how to organize the gestures. The main choices seem to be to order by form, as words are presented alphabetically in a dictionary, or by meaning, as words are presented in a thesaurus.

There is, however, no standard ordering of gestures by form. There have been attempts to devise notation systems for gestures, sometimes derived from notations for sign languages, but none has become generally established.[66]

The alternative seems to be to attempt to list conventional gestures alphabetically according to the kind of "message" they are intended to convey: an emotion, directions, sarcasm, a challenge, etc. Organizing in this way has been plagued by the ambiguity of what is meant by "the message of a gesture," mixing labels for emotions, type of act (command, query, performative), words that typically accompany the gesture, and the meaning of the gesture in terms of a verbal phrase.

Another possibility used by Cláudio Basto in "A Linguagem dos Gestos em Portugal," 1938, and Desmond Morris in *Bodytalk*: *The Meaning of Human Gestures*, 1994, is to group gestures according to the most important part of the body that is involved in the movement. Typically within one such grouping the gestures are then arranged alphabetically by their "message."

Arranging by body parts allows homonyms to be placed next to each other; arranging by messages allows synonyms to be placed next to each other. Neither is a clearly better or even good option. Kendon, in his introduction to de Jorio's book, suggests that we follow the lead of de Jorio in using multiple indices:

> It is worth remarking that the view de Jorio has of how a gesture dictionary should be organized is well worth considering today. Of particular note is his attempt to construct complementary indexes of themes, meanings, and gesture forms. No modern attempts at gesture dictionary making have followed de Jorio's lead. All of them list their entries in terms of verbally formulated meanings, alphabetically arranged.
>
> Gesture dictionaries have their entries arranged in this way partly because no system of writing gestures down as forms of action has ever been agreed upon. Even if it were, however, there would still be problems, as the experience of creating sign language dictionaries has taught us in recent years. ...
>
> It may be that what makes the problem of making a dictionary so difficult is that the idea of a *dictionary*, analogous to a lexicon of words in a spoken language, provides the wrong model. Perhaps it would be better if we were to

---

[66] One of the earliest is due to Garrick Mallery and others in Mallery, *Sign Language among North American Indians Compared with that Among Other Peoples and Deaf-Mutes*, 1880, pp. 544–552. Sparhawk, "Contrastive-Identification Features of Persian Gesture," 1978, is an attempt to "[chart] gestures according to gross articulatory similarities and comparison of similar gestures for contrastive-identificational features." Calbris, *The Semiotics of French Gestures*, 1990, presents detailed appendices for how to organize a dictionary of gestures according to "relevant physical features." See also Isabella Poggi and Marina Zomparelli, "Ipotesi sul Lessico dei Gesti," 1987 for a proposal about what should be in the entries in a dictionary of gestures.

think of gestures rather as we think of plants when we go to construct a flora. According to this idea gestures would be organized into families according to their own characteristics and then indexes complementary to one another would be supplied, so that we could look up gestures from many different points of view. This is the direction in which de Jorio's own attempt seems to point us.[67]

But even if we give multiple indices, we still have to make a decision about the initial order of presentation of the gestures.

In our gestuary the initial ordering is mostly by meanings. However, there are no standard descriptions of meanings of gestures. The large categories of meanings in which we group the gestures are as much given by context of use as by any ordinary notion of verbal meaning. A number of gestures are distinctive in that they can be combined simultaneously with many other gestures, and we group those together at the start because of the importance they have in amplifying or modifying other gestures. In total, there are 423 entries in our gestuary (and we're still adding more as we note them).

For each entry we list homonyms, along with synonyms and gestures of related meaning or form, and we try to make those relations clearer in the schema that introduce the sections. That cross-indexing is at best partial, especially in the current draft in which not all of the gestures are illustrated. In addition, we include the following indices of the gestures:

- Gestures used principally by children.

- Gestures that can be used by only one or a certain combination of genders.

- Communicative postures.

- Stylized emotions.

- Active reciprocal gestures.

- Responsive reciprocal gestures.

- Gestures that involve touching someone.

- Gestures that involve a standard object.

- Gestures listed by the principal body part used in the gesture.

- Gestures listed alphabetically by their titles.

There are many different ways gestures can be related to one another or grouped by meaning and context of use. Our choices here not meant to be definitive, much less exhaustive. What we present is an essay, an attempt, that we hope will elicit deeper understandings and better orderings from others.[68]

---

[67] In de Jorio, 1832/2000, pp. lviii-lix.

[68] We hope to create an electronic version of this gestuary that will incorporate templates for ordering gestures in any manner a reader might wish. The cross-referencing to homonyms,

Dictionary-making compared to gestuary-making

The introductory essay "Making a Dictionary: Ten Issues" in *Making Dictionaries* by William Frawley, Kenneth C. Hill, and Pamela Munro is a clear exposition of how makers of dictionaries of indigenous languages deal with problems similar to those we describe above.

In that same volume, Joseph E. Grimes in "Lexical Functions as a Heuristic for Huichol, 2002," grapples with what to make an entry:

> We do not actually define words; we define senses of words.* Each sense in which a word is used has its own definition. It may have much in common with definitions for other senses of the same word, but in its totality no definition covers accurately any of the other senses.**
>
> footnotes:
> * As a matter of fact, it is not senses of words but senses of lexical items, which may be parts of words, full words, or phrases.
> ** If it proves impossible to write definitions for two senses with enough in common to show the meaning connection between them, it is likely that we are dealing with homographs rather than polysemy. p. 75

What can Grimes in the second footnote mean by "show the meaning connection between them"? In our work we have found that idea too vague to be useful, which is why we simply treat different "senses" as different gestures, comparable to what he might call a different word. But it seems that his notion of word is "meaningful sound" not "sound + meaning." Later in that paper he proposes an approach similar to what we have adopted:

> We are all familiar enough with the notion of a thesaurus that we can readily imagine a vast web of associations among words. Lexical function theory suggests that these associations are of different kinds and have more structure than one might suspect, enough that we can use the associations themselves to track down other words and senses. They can be specified more precisely than the "have something to do with each other" relation that is behind the typical thesaurus. We now recognize that the entire vocabulary of a language is tied together by many different but identifiable kinds of ties—lexical functions—into a highly structured superthesaurus.
>
> These conventional relations among lexical items are part of every language, a standard feature of the lexicon that every native speaker knows implicitly. They should at least be reported, and the dictionary is the logical place to do that. p. 77 [69]

synonyms, and related gestures will be by links given by small copies of the headshots of those gestures.

[69] See Epstein's "Language-Thought-Meaning," 2015, for a discussion of such associations and how they can be tracked.

An Annotated Bibliography of Collections of Conventional Gestures

Collections of gestures have been published as books or articles in a wide range of scholarly publications, including linguistics, folklore, anthropology, psychology, psychiatry, and sociology. They have often appeared in little-known publications with very small distribution. In order to broaden awareness of the range of scholarship, we annotate here the books and articles we have found in which at least a few gestures are described. This also gives us an opportunity to discuss more fully some of the issues raised in the essay. We also list a few works whose titles led us to believe they would be about conventional gestures but that we found not to be of relevance to our work in the hope that this information will help others judge what they want to read.

At one time we thought we could give a comprehensive bibliography of all such collections. But time, patience, funds, and limited library access has kept us from doing all we had hoped. In particular, we do not include works from antiquity to about 1800; for references to those, we suggest the historical overview that Adam Kendon provides in *Gesture: Visible Action as Utterance*, 2004, and the articles listed in Jan Bremmer and Herman Roodenburg's, *The Cultural History of Gesture*, 1991. Nor have we tried to survey all collections that appear on the Internet because those do not seem to be prepared with sufficient thought to merit such an analysis (see the annotation for the one by Charlene Wu, 2011, below).

Unless noted otherwise, each work contains only written descriptions of gestures.

ADAMS, Thomas W.
1987 *Body English: A Study of Gestures*
    Scott, Foresman and Company.

This is a textbook for students learning American English. It is divided into 10 units corresponding to parts of the body. There are two indices. The first is a semantic or speech act index, with listings of gestures under headings such as "Achievement," "Agreement," "Anger," "Fulfilling expectations," "Requests." The second is by an expression that either describes or names the gesture such as "to bite one's nails." Gestures are not indexed by accompanying verbal expressions.

Each unit describes five body language items with language exercises based on those. The gestures are illustrated, with little indication of movement. Context and meaning are made clear. Some of the movements are conventional gestures, some are simply physiological reactions (to stand with one's mouth open in surprise), and some are stylized emotions. They all have in common that they can be correlated to an English phrase that a teacher can use to teach students English. The descriptions of the gestures and the drawings are not sufficient by themselves to learn how to duplicate most of the gestures but are sufficient for a class taught by someone who can illustrate the gestures.

No indication is given for how the gestures were known by the author, but the default in such cases for language teaching is that the author knows the material first-hand.

ALSOP, Stewart
1960 How to Speak French without Saying a Word
      Saturday Evening Post, Dec. 24–31, pp. 26–29.

The author reports on 9 conventional gestures he learned with the French underground during "several months" in World War II. Each is illustrated and explained.

AMADES, Joan
1957 El Gest a Catalunya
      Annales del Instituto de Lingüistica, Universidad Nacional de Cuyo (Mendoza, Argentina), vol. VI, pp. 88–148.

Because this is difficult to obtain and because many of us find it difficult to translate from the Catalan, we include a translation of the entire introduction here provided to us by Kathleen McNerney, a scholar and translator of works in Catalan.

Gestures in Catalonia
Ever since I became interested in the ethnology of language, gestures have drawn my attention and awakened a special curiosity in me, above and beyond any other aspect of linguistics. This particular interest has resulted in my effort to annotate as many gestures as I could, interpreting the concept in its broadest sense, taking note of all kinds of movements of fingers, hands and bodies, even infantile strokes and games. During these decades, I have gathered several thousand items in my file.

In trying to give form to the material, I ran across several problems. A good many of my entries were not really gestures of a linguistic type, so I discarded them since they belong with other, well-defined groups. Upon examination of truly linguistic items, it seemed that there were three types: general, individual, and indeterminate. The first, formed by gestures that point to a concrete, specific idea and are commonly used, belong to the pool of mute language (gesture only). In addition to those in general use, there are a number of personal gestures. Just as each speaker develops his/her own idiolect, so that there are as many "languages" as people on the planet, the same is true for gestures, even more so than any other aspect of language. Everyone has a special intonation and particular expression, which intensify when gesticulating is added. Individual gestures that cannot be considered as collective make up the second group.

Many people move continually while they are speaking; they cannot seem to express themselves without gesticulating, and the gestures are funny and expressive, underlining or emphasizing their ideas, and at the same time adding nuances to the conversation. The movements do not express a precise or concrete idea. This kind of gesture can be very expressive, and they form a third group of considerable quantity.

Evaluating the material has been labor-intensive, and I will only consider relevant those gestures that indicate specific ideas and are in general use, since they form part of the linguistic basis of the language studied. I have not included those personal items from the second group, nor the indeterminate ones from the third in spite of their great value. But I have included other items of ethnographic interest, such as gestures of oath-taking and conjuring, and others that fall into the category of children's games, of great ethnographic value. There are fewer documents in this category than in the others.

As far as the order is concerned, if the gesture had a name, I used it; if not, I classified them according to the idea they convey. Within that framework, they are in alphabetical order. My aim is to make known these gestures with linguistic properties which are most used in Catalonia. Since I know nothing written on this subject, I cannot offer a single bibliographic reference.

Joan Amades

Conservador del Museu d'Indústries i Arts Populars, Barcelona

Amades then gives 299 entries. The titles of the entries vary among a description of the movement of the gesture ("Lower one's head"), an explanation of its meaning ("To finish"), or a name of the gesture ("Dancing needle").[70] The entry then contains as needed a description of the movement and what the gesture is meant to convey. Almost all the entries are for conventional gestures, though a few are illustrative ("Violin. One imitates playing this instrument by stretching out an arm at shoulder level as if holding it while passing the other arm above it without touching it.") He takes a gesture to be a movement, associating different meanings to the same movement depending on context.

The entries are then followed by photographs taken by Miquel Carbó i Castany of 99 of the gestures. The photos are mostly of the principal part of the body that is involved in the gesture, though some show the whole body to give the placement of the hands. No movement is shown.

ARMSTRONG, Nancy and Melissa WAGNER
2003   *Field Guide to Gestures: How to Identify and Interpret Virtually Every Gesture Known to Man*
Quirk Books.

There are 108 entries for what are mostly conventional gestures. The authors take a gesture to be a symbolic nonverbal act that can have more than one meaning (p. 36). Each entry has the following sections: Usage and Origins; Region; Environment; Execution. The first part has a short description of the movement, comments on its meaning, and its etymology; the second part says where the gesture is used; the third gives the context of usage; and the last gives a detailed description of the physical movement. With some entries a sketch of the movement is given, while in a center color section each gesture is illustrated with one or more photographs. In both sketches and photos only the principal part of the body is shown, which can be

---

[70]   Abaixar el cap; Acabar; Agulla ballarina.

misleading: "OKAY" (# 18, our *A–OK*) is illustrated with the back of the hand shown, while it is the palm-side that is shown to the other person in the United States. The first 48 gestures are common to what they call "North America," though that seems to exclude Mexico; the succeeding ones vary in region.

The authors give no information about how they know the gestures or their etymologies other than their bibliography, which cites a few articles about specific gestures and some gesture collections of dubious reliability. Many of the entries are for gestures associated with sports or are known mainly to young people who are part of the current culture, particularly that of television programs that gave rise to short-lived gestures. We suspect this is the source for their entry for "Nose tap," which though they say is common in North America, almost none of our colleagues have ever seen:

> The side of the nose is tapped with the tip of the index finger. The nose tap gesture is done to imply collusion between two individuals, as if to say, "You and I have a secret that we won't tell anyone else, though others will try to sniff it out." p. 165

To evaluate their work we need to know more about the authors' background, most particularly where they have lived and their ages. Perhaps it is because they are women that the sketch they give for "The Butt Pat" (p. 41, our *Pat on the ass*) has one man reaching across to pat the buttock on the opposite side of the other man rather than the same side, which men would take not as a sign of approval but as sexual intimacy.

AXTELL, Roger E., illustrations by Mike FORNWALD
1991   *Gestures: The Do's and Taboos of Body Language around the World*
       John Wiley & Sons, Inc. Revised and expanded edition, 1998.

This is a book designed to sensitize American business travellers to differences in body language and customs around the world

Mixed among anecdotes with descriptions and comments on body language and customs, Axtell describes many conventional gestures from around the world, where a gesture is taken to be a symbolic action. At least one meaning for each movement is given along with an indication of where that movement has that meaning. Drawings accompany many of the descriptions.

In the acknowledgements, Axtell thanks a number of people from different countries and on pp. x–xi speaks of a questionnaire sent out to "150 embassies, consulates, honorary consuls, friends, and cross-cultural specialists around the United States asking for suggestions for changes to the first edition." He says on p. xv, "This book, then, results from an accumulation of more than ten years of research, including recent research visits to England, Germany, France, the former Yugoslavia, Greece, Italy, Hong Kong, Thailand, Malaysia, Indonesia, and the Philippines." But he also draws heavily on the work of Morris, 1994, and Morris,

Collett, Marsh, and O'Shaughnessy, 1979, and it is not clear what in this book is from Morris and what from Axtell and his contacts. Thus, the unreliability of Morris' work (see the annotations below) makes it difficult to judge what is reliable here.

Many fanciful etymologies are proposed. For example, of the "ear waggle" Axtell says on p. 34, "When one does this and flaps the hands back and forth, he is probably imitating the long, floppy ears of the donkey, an animal usually depicted as lazy and stupid." But many people we know have never encountered a donkey or even know that it has long, floppy ears. As etymology Axtell might be right, though absent a written testament to that effect by someone at roughly the time it first became popular we cannot imagine how one could know; as a comment on what people think who are using it, this is certainly wrong.

BANKS, Ann
1974   French without Language
       Harvard Today, vol. 181, pp. 4–6.

This is a review of the work of Laurence Wylie on French body language and culture. The last page has photographs and discussion of 7 French gestures, performed by Wylie and photographed by Rick Stafford. Compare Wylie and Stafford, 1977 (annotated below).

BARAKAT, Robert A.
1973   Arabic Gestures
       Journal of Popular Culture, vol. 6, pp. 749–787.

This is a collection of gestures, described both verbally and with photos, from what the author calls "Arabic" countries: Saudi Arabia, Lebanon, Jordan, Syria, Kuwait, Egypt. The scope appears to be mostly conventional gestures, with some body language.

Barakat does not describe how he collected the gestures. A few times he says that the lists are not complete because they do not include women's gestures and are only a representative selection of Bedouin gestures. But it's not clear that the list is complete even for Kuwait since he gives so few gestures for that country. He speaks of visiting some of the countries and interviewing informants in the U.S., but which gestures were obtained in which manner is not made explicit. Nor does he say whether he is a native of one of those countries or whether he speaks Arabic.

BASTO, Cláudio
1938   A Linguagem dos Gestos em Portugal
       Revista Lusitana, vol. 36, pp. 5–72.

In this paper Basto initiates a gestuary for Portugal. He describes his method:

> This analysis—a simple ethnographic sketch—is based on direct observation, but, in order to better clarify the movement, the meaning and the use of the gestures, I will present, from time to time, appropriate extracts from books—

particularly of a realistic aspect. These extracts clarify, document, and make it easier for the reader.[71]

His quotations from the literature are extensive.

Basto presents 59 gestures: 9 under the heading "Entire body" and 50 under "Head." They are a mixture of conventional gestures, stylized emotions, and communicative postures. Basto's list and description of ways to use the head and face to express attitudes and emotions are the most extensive and careful we have seen. The paper ends with the notation "To be continued," but we have been unable to locate any further collection of gestures he published that would complete this.

See p. 52 above for Basto's comments on the limitations of describing gestures verbally.

BAÜML, Betty J. and Franz H. BAÜML,
1975 *A Dictionary of Gestures*
The Scarecrow Press, Inc.

The authors describe the scope of their work:

> This dictionary contains primarily non-codified, non-arbitrary, culturally transmitted (semiotic) gestures.

We cannot understand what they mean by this since they include "Money" (our *Money*), which is purely conventional and surely arbitrary, as well as blushing.

They describe their methodology of collecting gestures:

> We have limited our collection to descriptions or depictions of gestures in verifiable sources. No gestures of solely our own observation are included.

Their source list is extensive and includes Henry Fielding's *Joseph Andrews* and Apollonius Rhodius' *Argonautica* as well as works of art. But, as we discuss in the annotation of Morris, Collett, Marsh, and O'Shaughnessy, 1979, the use of ancient art may be unreliable without further documentation.

The order of presentation of the gestures is given by the most significant body part subdivided alphabetically by meaning.

BRAULT, Gerard J.
1963 Kinesics and the Classroom: Some Typical French Gestures
The French Review, vol. 36, pp. 374–382.

The author presents a number of French conventional gestures.

> What follows is a representative list of French gestures culled from [Alsop, 1960, and Scherman, 1946] as well as from personal observation, followed by a brief commentary. p. 376

---

[71] Êste ensaio—simples esbôço etnográfico—baseia-se na observação directa, mas, para melhor esclaracer o movimento, o significado e o uso dos gestos, apresentarei, de quando em quando, apropriados recortes de livros—em particular, de feição realística. Êsses recortes esclaracem, documentam, e amenizam a leitura. p. 5

These are 21 entries with titles such as "Amused Amazement" and "Invitation to Eat." Each describes the movement and meaning of the title gesture, often with a comparison to an American one that is similar in meaning or form. Some entries contain discussions of additional gestures. The descriptions and discussions are clear and helpful, though one of the American gestures that he describes is unknown to us: "a person will sometimes make a rapid, sweeping, and slightly rising motion to the right with the right hand, the fingers and thumb being held together tightly. This gesture is sometimes accompanied by a whistle," which he says means "Hasty Retreat." He does not say if he is French or American. All the gestures in this work are analyzed and illustrated in Theodora M. Tsoutsos, 1970, which is annotated below.

Brault also compares the movements of French and Italian gestures:

> French gestures are characteristically simple and chopped, compared, for instance, with certain Italian hand movements which are generally executed with a flourish. p. 376

BREWER, W. D.
1951   Patterns of Gesture among the Levantine Arabs
American Anthropologist, 1953, pp. 232–237.

> The materials of this paper were collected during a residence of little more than a year in Beirut, Lebanon, when the writer was struck by the very obvious gesture mechanisms invariably used by the majority of the native population, as well as many semi-acculturated visitors in certain well-defined situations. This paper is the result of some rather random observations in Beirut, together with more formal work during the spring and summer of 1949 with a Damascene informant at the Foreign Service Institute, Department of State, Washington, D.C. During his work with this informant, the author was able to detect no significant differences between the important gesture patterns of Beirut and Damascus. No distinction is therefore made in the present paper.   p. 232

Brewer divides gestures into three groups in relation to speech:

> Group I.   Gestures with symbolic meaning which are used, and fully understood, independent of speech.
>
> Group II.   Gestures with pictorial meaning which usually occur in specific conversational situations and which might not be understood independent of speech.
>
> Group III.   Gestures with merely emphatic meaning which occur in specific conversational situations and which would be virtually incomprehensible independent of speech.   p. 234

He lists 10 gestures of Group I, none of which are common in the US. He lists 8 in Group II, but all of those seem to be conventional gestures that should go in Group I, for example, "Put right thumb back and forth across middle of right index finger, with hand held semi-clenched. Meaning: Symbolizes money and usually accompanies a phrase about money." Brewer then lists 3 gestures in Group III, one of which seems to be a conventional gesture, "Extend hands, palms held open and down, in front of chest, and tap the tip of each index ginger rapidly against its thumb. Meaning: A 'twin' gesture, this is used to emphasize the smallness of something."

BROIDE, Nitza
1977   *Israeli Emblems: Israeli Communicative Units: Emblem Repertoire of "Sabras" (Israeli Natives) of Eastern European descent*
        Doctoral dissertation, University of Tel Aviv.

We have been unable to obtain a copy of this, which other references say collects 118 Israeli emblems.

CALBRIS, Geneviève
1990   *The Semiotics of French Gestures*
        Translated by Owen Doyle, Indiana University Press.

This is a report and development of work done by the author elsewhere.[72]

This book describes verbally and depicts with photos and some drawings thirty-four common French "gestures and facial expressions that accompany or replace spoken language" (Preface), along with their verbal accompaniments. Apparently the gestures were all known by the author and were chosen because they used various types of movement, parts of the body, and places of the gesture in relation to the rest of the body.

A film was made of the gestures performed by the author, but no reference is given for how to obtain a copy. Then the gestures were shown to groups of French students from English classes with the sound turned off to see if the subjects could match the gesture to the verbal accompaniment or meaning on the list given to them. This method, however, has long been deemed to be inappropriate in the testing of recognition. As L. Kanner, "Judging Emotions from Facial Expressions," 1931, says:

> [A controlled vocabulary] opens the door to additional possibilities of suggestion and, to a considerable extent, of a more or less guessed and, in any event anticipated correlation between a given series of portraits and another series of words . . . [and curtails] the individual's own "linguistic inventiveness" . . . . The smaller the list (and the number of photographs), the easier is the correlation of words and pictures, . . . The presence of a term in the list does not exclude complete ignorance of its accepted meaning.

The author performed the same experiment with the same French gestures using subjects from Hungary and again with subjects from Japan and found that many of the gestures could not be understood by them.

---

[72] "Étude des Expressions Mimiques Conventionelles Françaises dans le Cadre d'une Communication Non Verbale," *Semiotica*, vol. 29, 1980, pp. 245–346; "Étude des Expressions Mimiques Conventionelles Françaises dans le Cadre d'une Communication Non Verbale Testées sur des Hongrois," *Semiotica*, vol. 35, 1981, pp. 125–156; *Contribution à une Analyse Sémiotique de la Mimique Faciale et Gesturelle Française dans ses Rapports avel la Communication Verbale*, Thèse de Doctorat ès lettres, Paris III.

Calbris also presents an analysis of the relation of form of movement to the meaning symbolized, which is critiqued in Kendon, "Abstraction in Gesture," 1992.

CALBRIS, Geneviève and Jacques MONTREDON, dessins de ZAÜ
1986   *Des Gestes et des Mots pour le dire*
       Clé International.

This book is apparently meant as an aid in teaching French language and culture to non-native speakers. Or perhaps it's meant to help teachers of French for non-native speakers. There is no indication how the authors know these gestures.

The book is a mixture of lots of different kinds of gestures. Some are certainly conventional and can be used without any speech. Others may be conventional but also accompany speech. Some are gesticulations. And some are body language. The examples of contexts they give are all short dialogues in which an asterisk marks where the gesture would be made.

There are over 150 entries. They are grouped according to their meaning, for example, "Reflection" and "Fear." In some entries there is one movement with different meanings; in others there is one meaning with different movements. There is a second alphabetical index in which the entry is listed by the key word in its title, for example, "Avoir l'*estomac*" is listed under "E". There is also an index with 76 entries in which gestures are listed by parts of the body.

There is a section called *Temps*; the word is ambiguous between "time" and "tense." Gestures are illustrated for:

near past (*passé proche*)
distant past (*passé lointain*)
future
prior to (*antériorité*)
after (*postériorité*)

Except for "future," none of these are names of a grammatical tense of spoken French. All the examples of the use of these are in dialogues, either amplifying or explicating what is spoken, or replacing a word or phrase in what is spoken. It is not clear whether these gestures can be used without speech. It is also not clear whether these gestures qualify as tenses, that is, whether they can be combined with other conventional gestures to time-mark those.

CANGELOSI, Don and Joseph Delli CARPINI
1989   *Italian without Words*
       Meadowbrook Press, Simon & Schuster.

This is a collection of 88 different Italian gestures, grouped semantically. Each is illustrated with a photograph; no indications of movement are given. Each gesture is labeled with what appears to be a verbal equivalent in Italian, with a translation into English. The authors, who are American, do not explain how they know the gestures.

CARDONA, Miguel
1954   Gestos o Ademanes Habituales en Venezuela
         Archivos venezolanos de folklore (1953–1954), Caracas, Universidade Central de Venezuela,
         Año II-III, tomo II, número 3, pp. 159–166.

Cardona describes and gives drawings of 22 Venezuelan gestures that he apparently observed personally. He is careful to give the context of use of each, paying particular attention to the appropriate social level.

CARPITELLA, Diego
1972   *Cineseca Culturales 1 Napoli*
         Rome. Accessed at <www.europeanfilmgateway.eu>
????   *Cineseca Culturale 2 Babaglia*
1981   Cinesica 1. Napoli. Il Linguaggio del Corpo e le Tradizioni Popolari: Codici Democinesici e
         Ricerca Cinematografica
         La Ricerca Folklorica, no. 3, Antropologia visiva. Il cinema. pp. 61–70.

The article (1981) is a description and analysis of the first film, scene by scene, with some comments about the second film. We have been unable to obtain a copy of the undated second film.

The author says the first film is meant to illustrate and investigate a book *La Musica Degli Antichi Investigata nel Gestire Napoletano* by Andrea de Jorio, 1832; we suspect that this is a misprint with "musica" in place of "mimica." A large portion of the film is of a traditional fertility dance, focusing on just one man. There is also a section in which certain gestures are performed in front of a group of students at an elementary school. The film is in black and white, the scenes are outdoors, and there is no sound: the article gives the dialogues that accompany the scenes.

CASCUDO, Luís da Câmara
1976   *Historia dos Nossos Gestos*: *Uma Pesquisa na Mímica do Brasil*
         Melhoramentos. Corrected edition, Global Editora, 2003.

This is an idiosyncratic listing of anything that involves movement that happened to strike the author's attention. The entries include (p. 21) "tapping your foot in rhythm" as synonymous with dancing; (p. 22), "closing the eyes"; and (p. 209) "to look—intermittently or fixedly." Each is accompanied by a short essay. Many of the descriptions of the movements are not clear enough for a person unfamiliar with them to duplicate.

COCCHIARA, Giuseppe
1932   *Il Linguagio del Gesto*
         Fratelli Boca, Torino.
         Published in a new edition 1977 by Sellerio editore Palermo with an Introductory Note by
         Silvana Miceli.

We have seen only the 1977 edition. The Introductory Note says this book was first published in Italy in 1932, but we have been able to find information about that printing. In the Preface, dated 1931, the author says that the book was written in

England for an English publishing company and translated by Federico Tollemache, but it is not clear whether the translation was from English to Italian or Italian to English.

The book is concerned with gesture generally. Particular conventional gestures are discussed as examples in several places. Separate sections are given for the conventional gestures "La mano di Fatma," "La mano in fica," "Le corna," and numbers. The author assumes that the Italian reader is familiar with the gestures and does not describe the movements; the only conventional gestures that are illustrated are those for numbers.

COOKE, Jean
1959   A Few Gestures Encountered in a Virtually Gestureless Society
    Western Folklore, vol. 18, pp. 233–23.

This paper lists 40 gestures, mostly conventional. Each entry has a short description of the movement, though mostly only enough for someone familiar with the gesture to recognize rather than to learn it, along with some idea of what it means.

The first paragraph says:

> The sources of the following gestures, unless otherwise stated, are personal observations and contributions solicited from friends at the International House, Berkeley, in 1957.

The International House is a student residence at the University of California, Berkeley, set up to facilitate intercourse between foreign and American students. Four of the gestures Cooke says are "Mexican." She adds personal reminiscences and hypothetical etymologies. She believes that several of the gestures are universal.

There are at least five we do not recognize or that are not common now. But there's no reason to think that these are American gestures rather than ones she happened to observe among international students.[73]

CREIDER, Chet A.
1977   Towards a Description of East African Gestures
    Sign Language Studies, vol. 14 (1977), pp. 1–20.

This paper contains a list of about 75 gestures that the author, an American anthropologist working in the tradition of Ekman and Friesen, 1969, 1972, collected during a two and one-half year sojourn in East Africa. The gestures were from four different tribes of two different linguistic groups; no reason is given for why these four groups were chosen. No explanation is given for how the gestures were collected, nor whether the author is a speaker of the languages of the groups.

At the end of the paper the author says which of the gestures are found in which of the groups. The list is so short that we suspect it doesn't cover a large part

---

[73] #4 Horns; #5 Knocking off of hats; #9 The Shanghai gesture; or thumb-to-nose; #13 Repeatedly stroking the lower lip with the index finger; #16 Tongue in cheek.

of the repertoire of gestures of even one of the groups. Moreover, in several cases a gesture appears to be a variation of another one, either a diminutive or emphatic. Of the gestures he describes about one-half are American gestures or slight variations of those. One gesture he describes seems to be physically impossible: "Lower lip pushes upper lip to cover nostrils."

CRITCHLEY, Macdonald
1939 *The Language of Gesture*
Edward Arnold & Co. Reprinted by The Folcroft Press Inc., 1970.

On pp. 90–91 the author lists 11 gestures "common in the Near East." No information is given for how the author knows these.

DAHAN, G. and J. COSNIER
1977 Sémiologie des Quasi-Linguistiques Français
Psychologie Médicale, vol. 9, no. 11, pp. 2053–2071.

The authors propose a repertoire of gestures they have obtained from informants: 12 students who are 20 to 30 years old. The gestures they are studying are those of France, but they do not say what region nor where the informants come from. They ask the informants—though they don't say whether individually or in a group—the following question:

> Certain gestures can say something without the need of speech. Can you show me all those that you know and tell me what they mean to you?[74]

They say that with this method they obtain on average 20 gestures per subject. The informants were videotaped.

The repertoire was completed by a similar method with 20 subjects aged 20 to 60 years old. Nothing is said about where the subjects come from, their occupations, or their background. They did not videotape these subjects but made schematic drawings of the gestures.

At the end they give a list of their repertoire of "quasi-linguistic" gestures, in total 143, given solely in terms of a label for each gesture, such as "Je ne sais pas" (I don't know), "J'ai faim" (I'm hungry), "Ça me barbe" ("That bores me"), "Mon cul!" (My ass!). In a very few cases the title is accompanied by a short description of the movement, apparently to distinguish it for French people.

The authors make various classifications of the gestures they obtain and do a statistical comparison on that basis.

The authors do not make available the videotapes or drawings, except for illustrations of 16 gestures. Nor, except as noted above, do they describe verbally the movements of the gestures. Perhaps the authors believe that readers from France will know the gestures from their titles.

---

[74] Certains gestes peuvent dire quelque chose sans avoir besoin de parler. Pouvez-vous me montrer tous ceux que vous connaissez et me dire ce qu'ils signifient pour vous?

D'ANGELO, Lou
1975   *How to Be an Italian*
     Price/Stern/Sloan

This is an amusing book for Americans, playing to their prejudices about Italians. In it the author gives pictures of 18 conventional gestures, all but one of which are clearly and apparently reliably explained (the explanation of the one on p. 57 we assume is a joke).

DE JORIO, Andrea
1832   *La mimica degli Antichi Investigata nel Gestire Napoletano*
     Fibreno, Napoli. Translated as *Gesture in Naples and Gesture in Classical Antiquity* by
     Adam Kendon with an introduction by Kendon, Indiana University Press, 2000.

This is the first dictionary of gestures in the sense of conventional gestures (rather than rhetorical flourishes). It was out of print for many years, and Kendon's is the first full translation of it (Mallery, 1880, translated parts of it and reproduced some illustrations). Kendon contributes a useful essay as introduction, along with footnotes and an extensive bibliography.

Perhaps the clearest statement de Jorio makes about what he considers to be a gesture is:

> There are two aspects in terms of which a gesture or, that is to say, a well-
> defined movement or positioning of any part of the body can be considered:
> the manner by which the movement, position and arrangement of the hand,
> the fingers, etc., is physically executed, and the idea that is attached to it. p. 31

The scope of his work is made clear in the presentation of gestures and the discussions: Neapolitan conventional gestures of his time. At no point does he assume that a gesture has a meaning that can be easily translated into Neapolitan Italian.

De Jorio takes a gesture to be a symbolic movement, but it may have more than one meaning:

> A gesture may have one meaning, or it may have more than one meaning, as is
> also found for words in any language . . . . p. 32

> [section heading] *Some modern examples to show how a given gesture may be
> explained differently according to the subject of the situation in which it occurs.* p. 36

Each discussion of a gesture has a clear description of the movement, variations of it including emphatics, and comments relating it to other gestures. For example, on p. 177 one entry is:

> *Hitting oneself on the forehead with the palm of the hand.* Striking oneself on
> the forehead with a single blow with the extremity of the palm of one hand when
> some disappointment has befallen us, perhaps means that one is hitting one's
> thoughts (see section) for not having guided one properly in one's business.

The varying degrees of violence with which one hits the forehead expresses the greater or lesser intensity of the annoyance of one's experiences.

De Jorio's first motive for studying conventional gestures was to find a way to better understand movements depicted in ancient art, such as friezes, statuary, and vases; and for many of the gesture entries there are discussions about that.[75] At the end of the dictionary part of the book there are a series of illustrations showing gestures used in scenarios, along with extensive discussions of those.

It is difficult to give a good count of how many conventional gestures de Jorio presents, but there are surely more than 200. He gives three indices of them by title, by principal body part, and by meanings. See also our comments and quotations from this work on pp. 40–41 and p. 55 above.

De Jorio and others have commented that Neapolitan gesturing is much richer than gesturing in "northern" regions. Nothing we have seen suggests that Neapolitans have significantly more conventional gestures than American or other cultures. De Jorio, pp. 91–94, accounts for the difference by saying that Neapolitans are more expressive and given to hyperbole; Joan Acocella in "The Neapolitan Finger," 2000, p. 54, suggests that the difference is principally that Neapolitans consider gesturing an art form. At one time we thought the difference might be due to the more extensive grammar of Neapolitan gestures (see Section IV.F above). But Meo-Zilio in "Consideraciones Generales sobre el Languaje de los Gestos," 1960, notes that the Uruguayan system of gestures has the same grammatical resources while:

> The Uruguayan (and, in general, the Rio Platan) can be considered intermediate between Nordic peoples and southerners: more expressive than the former and more moderate than the latter. Such moderation does not refer so much to the richness of available gestures, since it can be said that almost the whole gamut of southern gestures are known, as to the employment (frequency, amplitude of movement, energy, etc.) that makes the same.[76]

Efron, 1941/1972, demonstrated and Wylie, 1977, also comments (see below) that Italians use gestures that encompass greater space than Americans.[77]

DEVEREUX, George
1949 Some Mohave Gestures
      American Anthropologist, n.s. vol. 51, pp. 325–326.

---

[75] See our discussion of the difficulty of interpreting ancient work in light of current gestures in the annotation for Morris, Collett, Marsh, and O'Shaughnessy, 1979 below.

[76] El uruguayo (y, en general, el rioplatense) puede considerase como intermediario entre los pueblos nórdicos y los meridionales: más expresivo que aquéllos y más moderado que éstos. Tal moderacíon no se refiere tanto a la riqueza de gestos disponibles, puesto que puede decirse que conoce casi toda la gama de los gestos meridionales, como al empleo (frecuencia, amplitud de movimento, energia, etc.) que hace de los mismos. p. 226

[77] Kendon, *Gestures*, 2004, pp. 349–354, offers a causal analysis of why Neapolitans gesture more amply.

The author presents some gestures he "happened to observe in the course of conversations dealing with other topics." Some are speech markers. There are at most 7 conventional gestures, including counting. Each is explained with an English phrase or a word, and the movement is very briefly described.

DIADORI, Pierangela
1990   *Senza Parole*   [100 Words]
      Bonacci editore.

This is both a study of Italian gestures and a textbook for non-Italians to learn Italian gestures and the Italian language.

Diadori delimits the class of gestures by excluding: ones that can be recognized by foreigners, such as "to eat," and "to drink," technical gestures that are used by a specialized group, sign language, ritual language, body language, and speech markers.

The 100 gestures that we present here have been chosen because they are:
—Conventional, that is, they have a universally accepted meaning within the
      Italian culture;
—Symbolic, that is, they indicate ideas, moods, etc., or in any case are not
      clearly related to their meaning and in this way are not immediately
      intelligible (understandable) to people from other cultures;
—Explicit, that is, they contain a message that the individual wants to transmit
      consciously;
—Schematic,that is, they represent something by choosing only some
      of its most obvious aspects.[78]

The entries for the gestures are grouped into the following sections:

Social conventions
      Salutation to initiate contact
      Salutation to conclude contact
      Congratulations
Emotional states and feelings
Action Schema
      Actions with respect to ourselves
      Actions with respect to others
      Actions with respect to us and others

---

[78] I 100 gesti che presentiamo qui sono stati scelti in quanto:
      —convenzionali, che hanno cioè un significato universalmente accettato all'interno della
cultura italiana;
            —simbolici, che indicano cioè idee, stati d'animo, ecc., o comunque non sono chiaramente
            riferibili al loro significato e quindi spesso risultano incomprensibili a persone di cultura
            diversa;
            —espliciti, cioè contenenti un messaggio che il soggetto vuole trasmettere consapelvolmente;
            —schematici, che rappresentano cioè qualcosa scegliendo solo qualcuno dei suoi aspetti più
            evidenti; . . . p. 14

Questions and answers
    Questions
    Answers
Opinions
    Showing the characteristic of someone
Descriptions
    Showing what's done (facts)
    Showing things or concrete elements
Insults

Each entry for a gesture has: a title that describes the movement of the gesture; a schematic cartoon of the principal part of the body involved in making the gesture with movement indicated; a brief "definition" of the gesture, which is a short phrase giving the meaning of the gesture; sometimes an indication of the context of use of the gesture; an indication if the gesture is formal, informal, or vulgar; one or more phrases in Italian that accompany and/or can be substituted for the gesture. Sometimes a definition is not given when the accompanying phrase(s) are clear enough.

A gesture is taken to be a movement with a specific meaning. For example, the movement of shaking hands is listed as two different gestures: one for saying farewell (#7) and one as a way to give congratulations (#12).

Following the presentation of the gesture entries, there is a section of teaching activities. This includes many photographs of gestures in use, advertisements, newspaper articles that mention gestures, and literary quotations that talk of gestures.

DOMINIQUE, Nilma Nascimento
2008a *Emblemas Gestuales Españoles y Brasileñas: Estudio Comparativo*
    Biblioteca Virtual redELE; Red Electrónica de Didáctica del Español como Lengua Extranjera. Accessed at <http://redined.mecd.gob.es/xmlui/bitstream/handle/11162/76274/00820103006785.pdf?sequence=1> on August 1, 2013.

This is a comparative analysis of Spanish and Brazilian emblems. The collections of gestures the author used for the basis of the comparisons are Meo-Zilio 1980–1983; Gelabert, Gifre,TD-Guach, and Mestre 1990; Mancera 1990; Cascudo 1987; and Rector and Trinta 1986. But most of the research is based on her own investigations.

The regions where the author interviewed informants were Salvador in Brazil and Madrid in Spain. She chose the former because that was where she was born and raised; she chose the latter because that was where she studied for her doctorate. She describes the regions of these cities and their populations and says that, because in both there are large numbers of immigrants (in Salvador internally from other parts of Brazil), she chose only those who were born in these cities or were brought there before age 10. She notes that in Salvador there is a strong African influence and heritage.

Her informants were classified into 3 age groups (20–34, 35–49, 50–)
and 3 levels of education (primary, secondary, university). Yielding 9 possibilities,
she took 3 men and 3 women for each group and had 54 informants for each city.

Each informant was interviewed separately, using a questionnaire that she
devised, which she reproduces on pp. 61–67. It has 132 questions divided into
sections according to the classifications she gives. There are two types of questions.
The first type asks the informant to produce a gesture.

"What gesture(s) would you use for . . . ?"
Then a message is given, e.g. "to avoid responsibility" or "to study".

"How would you express gesturally the following sensations or feelings?"
Then a message is given, e.g., "To see."

Among the messages is "Suicide." The second type asks whether the informant
recognizes a gesture.

"What do the following gestures indicate?"
Then either a drawing was shown or the gesture was performed;
in this printed questionnaire the movement of the gesture is
described verbally.

She lists 132 separate gestures in her analysis of the interviews and gives a statistical
analysis for each one concerning who recognized the gesture, and more.

DOMINIQUE, Nilma Nascimento
2008b Inventario de Emblemas Gestuales Españoles y Brasileños
Language Design, vol. 10, pp. 5–75. Accessed at
http://elies.rediris.es/Language_Design/LD10/LD_10_01_Nilma_Pazeado.pdf, August 7, 2013.

This is a comparison of conventional gestures used in Spain and Brazil. It is drawn
from the author's work Dominique, 2008a, annotated above.

There are 44 entries, some with multiple gestures discussed or illustrated. Each
has at least one photograph of the gesture being performed. The photographs are in
color, which is even more distracting than the usual problems with photos of gestures,
but this problem can be overcome by printing the article in black and white. Sometimes the photograph has an indication of movement drawn on it.

A written description of the movement of the gesture is given. The facial
expression is not described verbally, though in many it is clear that the facial
expression is a crucial part of the gesture.

One or more examples of verbal contexts in which the gesture might be
inserted are given, in Spanish for the Spanish gestures, in Portuguese for the
Brazilian ones.

A verbal equivalent, in Spanish for the Spanish gestures, in Portuguese for the
Brazilian ones is listed. This is followed by a description of the use or meaning of
the gesture plus further observations.

As an example, there is an entry "HARAGÁN, ser," which is a Spanish phrase meaning "to be lazy," for a gesture that is Brazilian and not Spanish. The examples of context are given in Portuguese:

> What a great (easy, comfortable) life!
> It's a good life
> He won the lottery and now lives this way . . . [79]

The verbal equivalent, given in Portuguese, is:

> To be a "good life"
> To have a great (easy, comfortable) life [80]

Its use or meaning is given in Spanish:

> Indicates that someone has a good life, full of pleasures.[81]

An observation is added in Spanish:

> Sometimes, depending on context, it has a negative connotation, since it indicates that the person the gesture referred to doesn't like to work.[82]

EASTMAN, Carol M. and Yahya Ali OMAR
1985   Swahili Gestures: Comments ("vielizi") and Exclamations ("viingizi")
        Bulletin of the School of Oriental and African Studies, University of London, vol. 48,
        pp. 321–332.

The authors discuss 21 conventional gestures that they say are emblems "used by Kenya coastal Swahili speakers." Of these, two are noted to be used only by women. Each is related to a specific Swahili word or phrase, and a short description of the movement is given along with the meaning and context of use. No mention is made of how the authors know these gestures. They cite an earlier paper by A. Claessen presented at a meeting that discusses many of these gestures, but we cannot find any information about the publication of that presentation.

EFRON, David, illustrations by Stuyvesant VAN VEEN
1941   *Gesture, Race and Culture*
1972   Mouton, The Hague. This is an expanded version of *Gesture and Environment*, King's
        Crown, New York, 1941. Spanish translation, *Gesto, raza y cultura*, Ediciones Nueva
        Visión, Buenos Aires, 1970.

This is a comparative study of the use of movements accompanying speech by Eastern European Jewish immigrants and Southern Italian immigrants in New York City. Efron defines a class of gestures in terms of several subclasses:

---

[79] Que vidão!, Ele é um (vida boa), Ganhou na loteria e agora vive assim . . . .
[80] Ter um vidão.
[81] Indica que alguien lleva una buena vida, llena de placeres.
[82] Algunas veces, dependiendo del contexto, tiene connotación negativa, pues indica que a la persona a la que se refiere el gesto no le gusta trabajar.

The "meaning" of the gesture is "objective", and the movement may be (a) *deictic,* referring by means of a sign to a visually present object (actual pointing), (b) *physiographic,* depicting either the form of a visual object or a spatial relationship (*iconographic* gesture), or that of a bodily action (*kinetographic* gesture), (c) *symbolic* or *emblematic,* representing either a visual or a logical object by means of a pictorial or a non-pictorial form which has no morphological relationship to the thing represented. p. 96

Note that his term "emblematic" covers only a part of this class.[83]

Efron describes his basic methods:

The investigation was carried out by means of a fourfold method, namely: (1) direct observation of gestural behavior in natural situations, (2) sketches drawn from life by the American painter, Mr. Stuyvesant Van Veen of New York City, under the same conditions, (3) rough counting, (4) motion pictures studied by (a) observations and judgments of naive observers, and (b) graphs and charts, together with measurements and tabulations of the same. p. 66

The motion pictures he speaks of were made by him. If we understand correctly, Efron spoke Yiddish, the language of the Jewish immigrants they were studying, and van Veen spoke Italian, the language of the Southern Italian immigrants they were studying. Van Veen contributed sketches of the movements, particularly the conventional gestures.

Efron's definition does not require a gesture to accompany speech, but his methodology was to observe gestures only as they occurred with speech, although he says (pp. 129–130) that they did note symbolic gestures for Southern Italians in New York City when they were not speaking.

Much of what Efron studied is what we call speech markers. But in an appendix, "A Short Dictionary of Southern Italian Descriptive and Symbolic Gestures Drawn by Professor Stuyvesant Van Veen," he and van Veen catalogue conventional gestures of that culture. The appendix contains 148 separate gestures, if a gesture is defined as a symbolic movement, since some have several meanings.[84] Each gesture is accompanied by a short description (see the examples on p. 21 above).

Efron concludes:

---

[83] On pp. 97–98 he traces the history of the study of roughly the larger class of gestures to Cicero. On p. 95 he traces the use of the term "emblem" to Francis Bacon.

There is a much older tradition dating to Quintillian in which "gestures" are understood as those physical movements that can be used as rhetorical flourishes to accompany public speaking. See, for example, Albert M. Bacon, *A Manual of Gesture,* 1881. Kendon, "Current Issues in the Study of 'Non-Verbal Communication'," 1981, pp. 28–29, discusses that tradition.

[84] Though 151 are listed on pp. 201–226, three are repetitions of earlier ones. Of these, only 30 are recognizable as American gestures now, even counting emotional reactions and cases where we use two hands instead of the one used in the picture: 3, 11, 13, 17, 27, 28, 31, 37, 41, 50, 53, 54, 56, 60, 79, 83, 84 (we use two hands), 94 (we use two hands), 98, 99, 101, 104, 108, 120, 127, 134, 141, 142, 144, 146.

> Like the ghetto Jew (and the American of Anglo-Saxon descent for that matter),
> the "assimilated" Jew has no system of "emblematic" gestures. The only truly
> symbolic movement which he uses rather frequently in conversation is the
> "American" thumbs-down gesture, signifying rejection or condemnation of
> an idea, an action, or a person.

This may be true for the Jews he studied while they were speaking. But from our
knowledge of people who lived at that time and from our observation of movies of
that period, the "American of Anglo-Saxon descent" as well as assimilated Jews had
a rich repertoire of conventional gestures as well as speech markers.

FATEHI, Kamal
1996 *International Management: A Cross-Cultural Functional Perspective*
      Prentice-Hall.

In a chapter on international communication, a table of 14 conventional gestures is
given. One entry, for example, is "Crossing first two fingers," which is said to mean
in the United States "Good luck!" and in Taiwan "No smoking!" The author does
not say how he knows the gestures.

FELDMAN, Sandor S.
1959 *Mannerisms of Speech and Gestures in Everyday Life*
      International Universities Press.

This is a psychiatric approach to understanding gestures. The section "Gestures"
takes up about one-third of the book. It is not clear what the author considers to be
a gesture.

> The "mannerisms of speech" should include gestures and all kinds of bodily
> movements which accompany, augment or substitute for speech. Gestures are
> conveyed by one person to another in visual, tactile, and (rarely) olfactory ways.
> p. 197

He does not distinguish between symbolic and non-symbolic movements,
having sections on "Playing with the ring on the finger and with the handbag,"
"Mannerisms of dressing the hair," "On tickling and ticklishness," as well as on a
number of conventional gestures such as "Sticking out the thumb" and "Crossing the
fingers." Not all of the latter are American gestures, for he includes "Fica" ("fig")
and "Index finger placed alongside the nose," which as far as we know were not
American gestures of that period.

One gesture he describes is so different from any we have encountered that it is
worth noting:

> Once more I return to my native town and to the gang of boys to which I
> belonged, between six and eight years of age.
>   Whenever the boys were on the outskirts of town and no other person
> (especially women) were in sight, and a boy stepped aside to urinate, another

boy would rush up close to him and start to do the same in such a way that the streams crossed each other. It was a "must" for the second boy to do so. When I asked one of the boys why they did this, he explained that by doing so an enemy would die. p. 273

There is no way to tell from this book if this was only a local gesture or was common to more of the country.

FLASCHKAMPF, Ludwig
1938 Spanische Gebärdensprache
     Romanische Forschungen, vol. 52, pp. 205–258.
1939 El Lenguaje de los Gestos Españoles
     Ensayos y Estudios, Berlin I/4, pp. 248–279.

We have consulted only the second of these, which is a Spanish version of the first. Starting with reflections about the nature of gesture, Flaschkampf lists several "movements which aid the expression of the speaker" and then gives 21 separate entries for conventional gestures from Spain. These are grouped into categories: "Surprise and wonder" (4); "Mockery, self-irony, offense" (8); "Offensive mocking gestures" (5); "Defense and negation" (1); and "Magical and obscene gestures" (3).[85] The title of each is a word or phrase in Spanish that apparently can be said with the gesture or is a verbal equivalent, except for the last three, which are titled with the name of the gesture, e.g., "The fig." Each entry contains a verbal description of the movement and a discussion of the meaning and use of the gesture. We are not told how Flaschkampf knows these gestures.

GELABERT, María José and Emma Martinell GIFRE; drawings by TD-GUACH and Josep Coll MESTRE
1990 *Diccionario de Gestos con sus Giros Más Usuales*
     Edelsa, Madrid.

This is a partial gestuary for Spain. In the preface the authors say that it is designed for students learning Spanish.

> We intend for this book to constitute an agreeable tool for personal use, whose knowledge aids the comprehension and learning of gestures that are seen daily. So we have proposed to limit ourselves to the *ninety-two gestures* we take to be most frequent, most general and endowed with a specific content. Therefore, we analyze expressions, gestures and postures that are known by all speakers, [whether they] have reflected on them or not on some occasion; not gestures exclusive to one group, to one age, or rude gestures that a part of speakers [in Spain] censure and avoid. . . .
>
>   The text is divided into *ninety two units*, each one of them relative to a content expressed gesturally. Each unit contains a title (word, expression,

---

[85] "Extrañeza y Admirición; Burla, autoironia, ofensa; Gestos de burla ofensiva; Defensa y Negación; Gestos mágicos y obscenos."

phrase) that is equivalent to the content of the gesture, with the description of
how and when the gesture is used, and with the reference to the corresponding
verbal expression. We indicate if the gesture goes with or without words,
or whether it substitutes for them. When it seems necessary to us, we have
prepared a short dialogue, or a description of a situation that explains when
the gesture is made.[86]

The authors say nothing about how they know these gestures, but from the
evidence of the entries we suspect that their method is similar to ours.

The entries for each unit are ample and clear. Each gives: a physical description of the gesture; a situation is described in which the gesture could be used and
how we are to interpret it; and often a context dialogue. Sketches are used to illustrate the gestures. The authors say they use sketches rather than photographs to
depict the gestures in order to show movement, though they would prefer to present
videos (see the annotation for Gifre and Ueda, 2002 below).

The 92 study units are divided into 10 groups:

Identification [pronouns, places]
Affirmation/negation
Quantity/size
Signs [hunger, thirst, . . .]
Evocation/description [to speak, can't hear, . . .]
Feelings/sensations [disgusting, what a surprise, . . .]
Situations [hello, goodbye, concentration, I'm ready . . .]
Orders/warnings [get up, sit down, silence!, . . .]
Jests/insults
Beliefs/superstitions

In some units more than one gesture is described, the distinct movements being taken
to be synonymous, so that considerably more than 92 gestures are discussed.

Some movements corresponding to physical states are listed, such as (unit 28)
"Hot" (waving one's hand in front of one's face and sweating), though for the most
part the authors present conventional gestures.

---

[86] Hemos pretendido que este libro contituya una amena herramienta de uso personal, cuyo conoci-
miento ayude a la comprensión y aprendizaje de gestos que se ven diariamente. Porque no hemos
propuesto limitarnos a los *noventa y dos gestos* a nuestro entender más frecuentes, más generales y
dotados de un contenido específico. Por lo tanto, analizamos expresiones, gestos y posturas que
conocen todos los hablantes, hayan reflexionado o no en alguna ocasión sobre ellos; no gestos exclu-
sivos de un grupos, de una edad, o gestos groseros que una parte de los hablantes censura y evita.

El texto está dividido en *noventa y dos unidades*, cada una de ellas relativa a un contenido
expresado gestualmente. Cada unidad cuenta con un título (palabra, expresión, frase) que equivale al
contenido del gesto, con la descripción de cómo y cuándo se hace el gesto, y con la referencia a la
expresión verbal correspondiente. Hemos indicado si el gesto va o no con palabras, o si las sustituye.
Cuando nos ha parceido necesario, hemos preparado un corto diálogo, o la descripción de una
situación, que expliquen en qué momento se hace ese gesto. p. 8

The authors also give an index that is designed to allow the reader to look up a gesture by specific phrases or expressions, which seem to be words that either accompany the gesture or give the meaning of it.

GIFRE, Emma Martinell and Hiroto UEDA
2002   *Diccionario de Gestos Españoles*
  Versión Internet. Ver. 2002/12/8// Accessos: 4/15218,
  <http://gamp.c.u.-tokyo.ac.jp/~ueda/gestos/index.html>.

This is a video supplement to the printed gestuaries Gelabert, Gifre, TD-Guach, and Mestre, 1990, and Takagaki, Ueda, Gifre, and Gelabert, 1998, with concordances for both. In 2003 while we were preparing this annotation the site became unavailable. Now in 2013 it is available again, but we're not sure that the videos are the same.

Each gesture is illustrated by a video that can be downloaded in which a person gives the movement along with a dialogue that is meant to accompany it. Various men and women perform the gestures.

There are 211 video clips listed under 88 semantic headings, and hence many of the semantic headings have several entries. In each, the part of the dialogue during which the movement is performed is noted in bold italic in the listing that has to be clicked. This helps to isolate the movement.

As an example, there are four entries for (1) "Approach":

"Come, come, listen to this."
  The motioning is with just the fingers.

"Come, come, approach, so I can tell you something."
  The motioning is more energetic and the whole palm faces
  the gesturer with the hand and palm moving together.

"Approach, approach, so you can hear better."
  The palm is moved downward toward the person.

"Approach, approach—you can see and hear better if you are closer.
Don't be embarrassed."
  The palms are upward and directed towards the body, and the
  woman uses her whole body and head together to motion the
  (unseen) person towards her.[87]

The small dialogue accompanying the gesture suggests when the one movement might be more appropriate than the other. But in the videos we cannot distinguish what is distinct to the gesture from what is idiosyncratic to the particular person in the video. For the third entry the woman moves her head a lot, which is not the case in the previous gestures; since we have to take the movement as a whole,

---

[87] Ven, ven, que te vas a enterar.
  Ven, ven, acércate, que te voy a decir una cosa.
  Acércate, acércate, y asi lo oirás mejor.
  Acercaos, acercaos, que lo vais a oír mejor si os ponéis mas cerca. No tengáis vergüenza.

it would seem the head movement is essential to that version. In the fourth version the whole body seems crucial. The concordance to (73) "Approach" ("Acérquese") in the printed gestuary Gelabert, Gifre, TD-Guach, and Mestre, 1990, is no help because that lists only the first gesture, which is presented both verbally and in a cartoon that is much more schematic than the video.

Another example is "I". Here there are videos illustrating: "Me?", "Not me", "It's me", "I'm called Fina", "It's my fault", "I'm sorry", and several others. Apparently, these are meant as variations on the same basic gesture, but the different contexts seem to have very different movements. With "I'm called Fina" the movement the woman makes with her head seems to be inseparable from the movement of the hand she makes to point to herself, but it is not clear whether that is essential to the gesture.

Still, this method approaches more closely how we learn gestures in ordinary life from a variety of situations and people using them. Used in a Spanish language course, as it is meant to be, the teacher could help students to learn not only how to recognize the gestures but also to perform them by providing corrections.

GREEN, Jerald R.
1968 *A Gesture Inventory for the Teaching of Spanish*
      Chilton Books, Philadelphia.

Green describes his method of collecting the gestures he illustrates:

> The information on peninsular Spanish gesture was collected in Spain during 1965–1966 from the following sources: (1) constant observation and recording of the nonlinguistic behavior of residents of Madrid, Spain, in the conduct of their daily activities—salespeople, civil servants, lecturers—*madrileños* engaged in every type of gainful employment and recreational activity; (2) regular attendance at scheduled classes at the Faculty of Philosophy and Letters of the University of Madrid during the academic year 1965–1966 provided the opportunity to observe and record the extralinguistic behavior of university students of both sexes before, during, and after class meetings, and to observe and record the gestural behavior of University of Madrid professors in the conduct of their classes; (3) fictional literature written by Spanish authors and published in Spanish in Spain—and elsewhere—since the conclusion of the Spanish Civil War (1939) was read (from one hundred and fifty to two hundred novels and collections of prose fiction), and complete and incomplete reference to gesture was recorded and documented; (4) dramatic literature . . . was examined for reference to gesture in the published stage directions; and (5) regular theater attendance during the 1965–1966 drama season in Madrid provided an opportunity to observe and record additional gestural information. pp. 23–24

The only gestures he says that he verified by native informants were incompletely described ones from fiction and drama. Nothing in what he says gives reason to believe that he interpreted correctly the gestures he saw or that he could distinguish between illustrative and conventional gestures.

HACKS, Charles, illustrations by Henri LANOS
1892 *Le Geste*
    Marpon & Flammarion.

This is about gesture in its widest sense: any human movement that someone, particularly the author, can find meaningful. A great deal of it is about body language and gesture in the theater. There is a discussion of some communicative postures on pp. 373ff, a discussion of how pronouns are shown with gestures on pp. 362–369, and a discussion of showing numbers with one's fingers on pp. 383–384.

HAMALIAN, Leo
1965 Communication by Gesture in the Middle East
    ETC.; a Review of General Semantics, vol. 22, pp. 43–49.

The author, who was a professor at the University of Damascus for two years, makes a number of generalizations about Arab gesturing based on observations he made "chiefly in Syria, but with frequent visits to Lebanon and Jordan." He discusses about 20 examples of conventional gestures, paying special attention to the difference in use between men and women. The meaning of those gestures is given with colloquial English phrases such as "Your offer is too low — go screw yourself, friend" and "Hello, you cool chick."

HAMIRU•AQUI
2004 *70 Japanese Gestures*
    translated by Alice Chang. Stone Bridge Press.

This is a compilation of Japanese conventional gestures to aid Americans visiting Japan. The author says in the Preface:

> Many people are of the belief that Japanese keep body action to a minimum
> when speaking, yet over 120 gestures are commonly used. Even after eliminat-
> ing those that will probably no longer be in use by the end of the next decade,
> 70 still remain. These are presented in this book.

Counting a gesture as a specific movement with a specific meaning, there are 93 conventional gestures given along with one body posture ("Line of vision," #26) and one game ("Jan ken," #59, rock-scissors-paper). Counting from 1 to 10 with one's fingers is illustrated. Notable is "Finger family" (#52): "Children express family members with their fingers. The thumb is the father finger. The index finger is the mother. The middle finger is the brother. The ring finger is the sister. The little finger is the baby."

    Each entry has at least one photograph, all of the same older man, Takafumi Hamada. The image is blurred except for the principal part of the body involved in the movement, which makes clear the crucial part of the gesture; though the position of the head and face are usually blurred, one can still distinguish the position and expression. Movement lines are drawn onto the photograph. Each entry also contains a description of how to perform the movement. The explanations of the meaning of the gestures are ample and clear, and the context of use is described. Contrasts are often made with American gestures in order to forestall misunderstandings.

The entry "Yes. No." (#2) contains a caution that illustrates the difficulty of identifying a gesture in one culture with what seems to be the same in another culture:

> As in the West, in Japan, one nods when saying "yes" and shakes the head sideways when saying "no."
>
> However, depending on the question, there are times when the English "yes" and "no" seem to be interchanged. (i.e.) "Aren't you going?" —"Yes (nodding the head) = ("Yes, I am not going.")
>
> In the West this question would be answered with a "No" and a shake of the head: "No, I'm not going." p. 11

HARRISON, Phyllis A.
1983 *Behaving Brazilian*
      Newbury House Publishers.

In a discussion of Brazilian customs, the author includes about a dozen of the most common Brazilian gestures, illustrated with photographs.

HAYES, Francis C.
1940 Should We Have a Dictionary of Gestures?
      Southern Folklore Quarterly, vol. 4, pp. 239–245.
1957 Gestures: A Working Bibliography
      Southern Folklore Quarterly, vol. 21, pp. 218–317.

The first paper has many references to published works from the late 1800s to 1940, especially in French and Italian. Hayes says,

> To date, I have collected about five hundred of what I have classified as "folk gestures". It should be possible to find at least one thousand more of this type alone.
>
> For a general classification of all gestures of mankind, I suggest the following:
>
> a. *Folk gestures*: nodding the head, shaking hands in greeting, shaking fist in defiance, pouting, biting the lips in vexation, lifting the eyebrows, etc.
>
> b. *Technical gestures*: the sign language of the North American Indian, or that of the deaf and dumb; semaphore signaling, umpire signaling, etc.
>
> c. *Autistic (or nervous) gestures*: "doodling", opening and closing objects carried in the hand, swinging watch chain, etc. p. 245

In the second paper Hayes describes some gestures, listing them as entries equal in status to books and articles, many of which lack notation for the author, editor, publisher, and/or year.

INDIJ, Guido
2006   *Sin Palabras*: *Gestiario Argentino* / *Speechless*: *A Dictionary of Argentine Gestures*
La Marca Editora, Buenos Aires. [Bilingual edition]

> Our aim is not to come up with a general theory of gestures, but to merely offer a classification of some gesticulations that have arisen from systematic (or ethnographic) observation of our peers in social interactions over the past year.
> In this respect, we have been in contact with actors, theater directors, anthropologists and linguists in order to attempt to identify, select, organize, decode and succinctly explain the use of a particular type of gestures: the *emblems*, or those which have a verbal equivalent in our culture. p. 50

> With the goal of exploring and promoting our gestural vocabulary and to optimize the interaction, we hereby present an initial repertoire of Argentine gestures: more than one hundred emblems that we consider the most recurring gestures in *our culture*: typical, valid signals of the Argentine being. p. 53

The book contains about 260 illustrated conventional gestures, including stylized emotions. Many of the gestures are not emblems, for the short word or phrase accompanying the gesture is clearly not a verbal equivalent. There is no suggestion that this is meant to be a complete collection of Argentine gestures, and some gestures are noted to be used by only a particular age or social group.

The main body of the text consists of separate entries. Each includes a title, a photograph of the gesture, a notation whether the gesture is obscene or a challenge, an explanation of what the gesture means and how it might be used, phrases that might be used with the gesture, information comparing the gesture to ones in other countries, and a verbal description of how to make the movement, all of which is translated into English. The English translation attempts to be colloquial American English, so that the translations of the phrases accompanying the gesture are often not literal translations from the Spanish. Many other gestures are noted in small panels in the introductory essay or are simply illustrated with a photograph and name-message along with others of that kind. For example, among the 23 "mimetic" gestures given on pp. 36–37, one is "Disparar–Shoot" and "Moco–Snot."

Some of the photographs have indications of movement drawn in, but generally the verbal description of the movement is needed to get an idea of how to do the gesture. Even so, there are a number of gestures that we could not figure out how to do and that we did not feel confident we could recognize.

The explanations of the meanings of the gestures are clear, apt, and insightful. Unfortunately, some include jokes that make it hard for us as Americans to decide what is serious and what is not. Nonetheless, this is an important and useful collection that can be used as a basis for comparison with that of Meo-Zilio, 1980–1983.

JOHNSON, Harold G., Paul EKMAN, and Wallace V. FRIESEN
1975 Communicative Body Movements: American Emblems
      Semiotica, vol. 15, pp. 335–353.

This is a compilation, discussion, and analysis of methodology on collecting American gestures. The authors list over 100 American gestures, but only by name or by a verbal equivalent of the gesture, with no physical descriptions of the gestures nor illustrations. We discuss this work in Sections II.B II.C, the beginning of Section III.A, Section V.I, and VIII.A.3.

JOHNSON, Kenneth R.
1971 Black Kinesics—Some Non-Verbal Communication Patterns in the Black Culture
      The Florida FL Reporter, vol. 9, nos. 1 and 2, ed. Alfred C. Aarons, pp. 17–20, 57.
      Reprinted in *Perspectives on Black English*, J. Dillard ed., Mouton, 1975, pp. 296–306.

The author discusses seven forms of non-verbal communication among Black Americans that are either conventional, such as rolling the eyes, or communicative postures, as well as including some body language. He draws comparisons with gestures of the dominant white American culture. Most notably different is the significance of turning one's back on someone:

> The action of turning one's back on another person in a group discussion or greeting always non-verbally communicates trust or friendliness. It also non-verbally communicates confirmation of what another Black has stated. p. 305

JOHNSON, Sahnny
1979 *Nonverbal Communication in the Teaching of Foreign Languages*
      Ph.D. Thesis, Indiana University.

This book is about nonverbal communication with some discussion of the importance of teaching it in foreign language courses. There is a good discussion of the nature of nonverbal communication and its relation to verbal communication.

There are good discussions of research about whether there are universal gestures (pp. 31–48) and about how we take gestures to be more truthful than verbal language.

Much of the text is about body language, but throughout conventional gestures, mostly from Japan and the Gulf of Arabia, are given as examples of particular points. In the last section, "Japanese NVC: Independent Gestures," 11 conventional gestures from Japan are presented.

> For the most part, our only source of information for the two cultures so far examined, Japanese and Gulf Arabic, has been extensive, personal interviews with representatives of those cultures. Our interview technique is entirely straightforward, attempting by detailed questioning to elicit areas of cultural clash with our own habits, followed by intensive examination of expected behavior patterns in the foreign culture. All information is rigorously cross-checked to assure reliability and to establish the extent of a practice. For the most part, the non-

deviousness of this approach has proved no problem as our subjects are primarily of the same age, class, and education level as the "target students," and most of them are rendered supportive and cooperative by having themselves experienced the same cultural bafflement that the project seeks to alleviate. p. 12

The conventional gestures are illustrated with black-and-white photographs showing the face(s) of the person(s) as well as whatever other part of the body is involved. No motion is indicated. Each of the photographs of the eleven Japanese gestures in the last section is annotated with a description of the movement, the context in which it is used, and its significance. Though the author says that she is examining emblems, which are supposed to have a short verbal equivalent, the titles she gives to the gestures fall into the full range of "messages" discussed in Section III.A above ("Excuse me, please let me pass through," "Embarrassment," "Perplexity, hesitation," "Food, eating, hunger"). Throughout Johnson notes whether the gesture can be used by only men, only women, or by both. A gesture, apparently, is meant to be a movement with at least one meaning but possibly more because the *Thumbs up* movement has only one entry but two meanings: "Boss, husband" and "Something is good or all right." See also Sebeok and Johnson, 1978, annotated below.

JOHNSON, Sahnny
1985   *Japanese Nonverbal Communication*
      Newbury.

Though referred to in several works, we have been unable to obtain a copy of this and are unsure if it was ever published.

JOSEPH, Jason and Rick JOSEPH
2007   *101 Ways to Flip the Bird*
      Broadway Books.

The authors give 101 distinct ways to do *The Finger*, each with an illustration and verbal description of the movement along with a discussion of the appropriate context. Mostly an attempt to be humorous, this book illustrates the variety of ways in which a single gesture can be done.

KANY, Charles E.
1960   *American-Spanish Euphemisms*
      University of California Press.

The author surveys the use of verbal euphemisms in Spanish-speaking countries of the Americas as well as New Mexico in the United States. In the discussion of some terms he notes that a gesture can be substituted or used with it. Forty-two of these apparently conventional gestures are illustrated in an appendix; the name of the illustrator is not given. The illustrations are of the principal part of the body involved with excellent indications of movement shown with a dotted line and arrow.

Each gesture has a number which at the bottom of the page indexes a word or very short phrase. Those words are in some cases the non-euphemistic meaning of the gesture, e.g., "matar" (to kill):

> Often the disturbing word [to kill] is avoided by the use of an appropriate gesture: that of drawing the index finger (or index and middle fingers), representing a knife, quickly across the throat; for example, [quotes from an Uruguayan source and a Venezuelan source].

In other cases the word or phrase is more like a title of the gesture or a description of what the gesture is meant to represent:

> The counteracting words *lagarto* and *contra* are used on other occasions when evil must be forestalled. It is often accompanied with this manual gesture: while the middle and ring fingers of the left hand are turned against the palm and held down with the thumb, the index and little fingers are extended to represent horns (see fig. 1). This is called *hacer (la señal de) los cuernos*, occasionally *hacer la contraguiña* (Venezuela, Colombia), from French *guigne* 'bad luck.' The extended fingers thus represent the horseshoe, often accepted as an emblem of good luck, and possibly a wishbone. Many silver or coral amulets represent a hand in this position. The gesture is sometimes made openly, and sometimes surreptitiously with the hand kept in the pocket. Since the natural purpose of the horn is to form a resistant or protective surface or even a tool or weapon, it becomes symbolical of resistance to or protection against evil influences. pp. 6–7

We have no idea how reliable this analysis is. Of his sources he says only:

> The illustrative material presented in this book derives from several sources: (a) many hundreds of informants whom I consulted on my numerous field trips to Spanish-American countries over twenty-five years, (b) scores of native consultants among students and instructors at the University of California, (c) the lexicographical works and authoritative monographs which I mention in the text, and (d) regional literature that confirms observed oral usage of the terms I discuss. pp. vi–vii

KAULFERS, Walter Vincent
1931   Curiosities of Colloquial Gestures
       Hispania, Vol. 14, pp. 249–264.

This is a collection of 58 gestures, where "gesture is defined broadly to include any external expressive movement of the body which accompanies, supplements, or replaces oral speech." All but 5 appear to be conventional gestures. Each entry contains a verbal description of how to perform the gesture along with a comment about its meaning and context of use.

Concerning his method and the provenance of the gestures, he says at the beginning in a footnote:

> The ensuing discussion is based primarily upon the writer's observations abroad,

supplemented by personal communication with natives of Spanish-speaking countries. p. 250

It seems then, though he does not say it explicitly, that the gestures he lists are from all Spanish-speaking countries except for those that he lists as being from particular countries (Spain 5, Mexico 10, Argentina 1, Porto Rico (*sic*) 2, South America 1). The unreliability of these, however, is commented on by the editor of the journal in a note at the end of the paper:

> The foregoing discussion approaches colloquial Spanish from a neglected angle. Any North American on his first visit to Spain has been surprised by unfamiliar gestures. That these are the same as described in this article is not certain, because it would seem that in many cases the word "Mexican" should have been used rather than "Spanish." p. 264

KAULFERS, Walter Vincent
1932 A Handful of Spanish
     Education, vol. 52, pp. 423–428

This is a story-like discussion of gestures used in Spain. The author describes 25 conventional gestures, usually with enough information about the movements that one could recognize and perform them.

KEY, Mary
1962 Gestures and Responses: A Preliminary Study among Some Indian Tribes of Bolivia
     Studies in Linguistics, vol. 16, pp. 92–99.

The author reports on a discussion held at a Summer Institute of Linguistics meeting on contacts with isolated tribes in Bolivia. "The discussion groups attempted to collect data on gestures and responses and to determine what part they might have in contacting a group of people when no mutual language is known."

Examples of gestures and responses from a number of Indian groups are described. The analyses are clear and cautious. Key points out on p. 96,

> When this tribe and other monolingual tribes were discussed, it was pointed out that any interpretation of their gestures and reactions was only tentative since the field worker did not know what was being said at the moment and what the emotion really was. While most of the observations of the Yuquis were given rather tentatively, it was also obvious that some of the observations were valid. For instance their enjoyment of the sugar was probably quite correctly reported.

The comments of the participants on the expressions of emotions in Indian groups suggests that stylized emotions may not be recognizable by people from a different culture. In particular, Key says on p. 96 that the Aymara people "are known to cry about things which don't seem to be sorrowful to us. They will cry freely when they ask for some favor." And of Movima women, she says, "At other times when they seem to be genuinely sorrowful, they talk *while* they are crying."

The most obvious conclusion was that emotions are not expressed in the same ways in different cultures. Our gesture language which is meaningful to us is as unintelligible to another culture as our verbal language is. p. 98

KING, W.
1949 Hand Gestures
Western Folklore, vol. 8, pp. 263–264 (in the section "Notes and Queries").

King lists a few gestures that he observed in and around the University of California, Berkeley. He writes:

The "bull sign" is the same gesture as the *mano cornuta*. The local gesture, made by closing the second and third fingers of the hand, leaving the index and little fingers extended, is used by the gesturer to indicate that his credulity is being tried. This symbol is supposed to represent the horns of a bull, and the gesture is often accompanied by the expression "Bull —[shit]."

Unfortunately, King does not say whether the gesture is made with the palm facing inwards or outwards. If it is inwards, then this interpretation is surprising, as at that time in other parts of the U.S. it was meant as a generally obscene challenge without any particular verbal equivalent.

KIRK, Lorraine and Michael BURTON
1976 Physical versus Semantic Classification of Nonverbal Forms: A Cross-Cultural Experiment
Semiotica, vol. 17. Reprinted in Kendon, 1981c, pp. 459–481.

The authors test various hypotheses about whether emblems have meaning independently of context (see the quote from them on p. 25 above). They presented 9 different emblems of the Maasai and Kikuyu, in various groupings of 3, to members of those different cultural/linguistic groups. The authors assume that gestures pertain to particular languages, rather than to cultures. For example, they say (p. 463) of the mouth point, "This is used to indicate an object or direction, very much as the finger is used for pointing in English."

KRISTEVA, J. and M. LACOSTE
1968 Bibliographie
Pratiques et Langages Gestuels, No. 10, Juin, 1968, pp. 132–149

This is an annotated bibliography of articles and books on the whole range of what might be considered to be gestures, restricted to works available in France in 1968.
There are 82 entries grouped into the following sections:

General theory of gesture
Anthropological and sociological status of gesturing
Psychology and pathology of gesture
Gestural systems
    Gestures in cultures
    Artificially created gesture languages

> Languages of monks
> The language of the Plains Indians of North America
> Gesture language of deaf-mutes

Gesture in art: representation and issues
>   Plastic arts
>   Dance
>   Theater
>   Cinema

Linguistic interpretations of gesture

American contributions: structural studies of body communication
>   Kinesic research
>   Proxemics [88]

Articles in our annotated bibliography that are annotated in this paper are: W. D. Brewer, 1951; Cocchiara, 1932; Efron and Van Veen, 1941; Hacks, 1946; Francis C. Hayes, 1940. Weston LaBarre, 1947, is included there, too, and is mentioned in our text but not in our annotated bibliography.

LEITE DE VASCONCELLOS, J., illustrations by Saavedra MACHADO
1917   A Linguagem de Gestos
>   *Alma Nova*, vol. 22, no. 21–24. Published as a separate volume by Imprensa de Manuel Lucas Torres, Lisboa.

In this study of Portuguese gestures, there are discussions of many kinds of gestures, including some conventional ones. The sections of the text are Preliminaries, Magical Gestures, Gestures Expressed in Literature, Caricatural Gestures, A Gesture of a Statue. Some of the gestures described in literature are illustrated, and in the section of caricatural gestures there are 12 illustrations of mostly conventional gestures, though the list also includes lighting a cigar, talking on the telephone, and shouting at someone.

---

[88]   Théorie génerale du gesture
Statut anthropologique et sociologique de la gestualité
Psychologie et pathologie du geste
Systèmes gestuels
>   Les gestes dan les cultures
>   Langages gestuels artificiellement créés
>   Langages des moines
>   Le langage des Indiens des Plaines d'Amérique du Nord
>   Langage gestuel des sourd-muets
Le geste dans l'art: représentation et problématique
>   Arts plastiques
>   Danse
>   Théâtre
>   Cinéma
Interprétations linguistiques de la gestualité
L'apport Américain: études structurales de la communication coporelle
Recherches kinésiques La proxémique

LEONE, Jay
1992 *Italian without Words: An Illustrated Guide to Italian Hand Gestures*
S.P.I. Books.

This is a short book illustrating and commenting on about 43 conventional gestures that the author, who is Italian-American, knows personally or has observed in Italy. The illustrations are by him.

MALLERY, Garrick
1880 *Sign Language among North American Indians Compared with that among Other Peoples and Deaf-Mutes*
U. S. Bureau of American Ethnology, Smithsonian Institution, Annual Report, vol. 1, 1879–1880, pp. 263–552. Reprinted 2011, Dover Publications.

This contains a partial dictionary of many signs used by North American Indians in what appears to be one or various sign languages current in North America in the 18th and 19th centuries, conceived of as an anthropological work. Mallery uses many illustrations and refers to a more complete dictionary, which we have not been able to locate. The work is notable for the care in which the methodology of collection and annotation of signs is described. Mallery makes an effort to understand whether the signing of North American Indians is a language, including what grammar it has. To do that, and also because he wants to show that signing is somehow natural and easily understood across cultures, he compares North American Indian signing to other systems of signs, including what he refers to as deaf-mute signs, as well as gestures of Greeks, Romans, and Neapolitans, using de Jorio's work (1832), parts of which he has translates or paraphrases and some of the illustrations of which he reproduces.

MANCERA, Ana María Cestero
1999a *Comunicación No Verbal y Ensenza de Lengua Extranjeras*
Arco/Libros, S. L., Madrid.
1999b *Repertorio Básico de Signos No Verbales del Español*
Arco/Libros, S. L., Madrid.

These two books comprise a single project.

The first gives what the author describes as the theoretical and methodological basis for including a study of non-verbal communication in the teaching of foreign languages, particularly Spanish. In doing so, she gives 14 examples of conventional Spanish gestures with information that could be presented in a lesson. Two of those are accompanied by photographs. All appear in the second book. The author does not tell us how she knows these gestures nor anything about herself.

The second volume is a collection of entries for gestures from Spain. Mancera says on p. 9 that these:

> . . . can be used in place of lexical or grammatical signs and particular verbal constructions, or to alternate or combine with them, in a more natural, fluid, and spontaneous interaction.[89]

The gestures are divided into three main categories:

Non-verbal signs with social use: those which we use in social interaction.

Non-verbal signs with structural uses in discourse: those which we utilize to regulate, control and organize communication in interaction.

Non-verbal signs with communicative uses: those which serve to have reference to specific notions, locations and ideas and to express states, sensations, feelings, etc.[90]

The entries are introduced by a verbal phrase or phrases, followed by a description of a context of use, a description of the movement, a photograph, non-speech sounds that might be made with the gesture, information concerning the space between the parties in the interaction, and information concerning the speed with which the gesture is made. The photographs contain many extraneous elements which make it difficult to pick out the schematic gesture. For a single word or phrase there may be more than one movement, with photo, described in an entry. The same movement may be described with a different verbal phrase and hence have a different entry. And "You?" (singular, question) on p. 71 is distinguished from "You" (not question, singular) on p. 69. At the end of the book there are two indices. The first lists all the gestures by section alphabetically under a general heading such as "Saludar" ("To greet") according to the phrase associated with the gesture. Thus, "Yo" and "Yo soy" ("I" and "I am") are listed since the gesture on p. 20 is introduced by both phrases, though "Ana" (a woman's name) that is given as a phrase for that gesture is not listed in the index. The second index is an alphabetical list of the gestures according to the phrase(s) associated with them; there are 389.

Some of the gestures in the second category—ones used with discourse—might be speech markers, but many appear to be conventional gestures. For example, the gesture labeled "Can I pass . . . ?, Could . . . ?, Can I . . . ?"[91] is presented in the first section under "To ask permission"[92] and is reproduced as a separate entry with a nearly identical photograph and similar description of the movement in the second section under the heading "To direct someone" with the phrases "Hey!, Excuse me! Sorry!,", which is distinguished only by the context of use, the latter in conversation in order to get a turn to talk.[93]

---

[89] . . . pueden ser usados en lugar de signos léxicos o gramaticales y de determinadas construcciones verbales, o alternar o combinarse con ellos, en la interacción communicativa más natural, fluida y espontánea.

[90] Signos no verbales con usos sociales: aquellos que usamos en la interacción social.

Signos no verbales con usos estructadores del discurso: los que utilizamos para regular, controlar y organizar la comunicación en interacción.

Signos no verbales con usos comunicativos: los que nos sirven para hacer referencia a determinadas nociones, ubicaciones e ideas y exteriorizar estados, sensaciones, sentimentos, etc.

[91] "¿Puedo pasar? , ¿Podría . . . ? , ¿Puedo . . . ?"

[92] "Pedir permiso."

[93] "Dirigirse a alguien". "¡Oiga!, ¡Perdone!, ¡Perdona¡"

The third section begins with gestures for pronouns: I, you singular, us, you plural, he/she, they.

The entries are clear, the written descriptions of the movements are ample and, as the author suggests, take the place of indications of movement in the photographs. The verbal phrases that accompany the entries, however, are misleading. They seem to be phrases that might be said in place of the gesture or perhaps with the gesture, but they are often much too specific. For example, on p. 71 Mancera introduces a gesture with the phrases "You? (singular), You? (formal), Are you Pedro? (informal), Are you Pedro? (formal), You have to do it"[94], while on p. 70 she has "You (singular)". For a gesture for picking out an object on p. 75, she gives the phrases "This is the new vase," "I want this doll,"[95] which seem to be more suggestions for how to incorporate the instruction of the gesture into a lesson for teaching Spanish than the meaning of idea of the gesture in any general way.

MARTIN, Peter
2003   How to Tell the French to Screw Off
    Esquire, July, p. 24.

Three French conventional gestures for telling someone to shut up, that what he or she is saying is "baloney," and to express extreme disbelief are illustrated with photos and descriptions of the movements.

McCORD, Charlotte
1948   Gestures
    Western Folklore, vol. 7, pp. 290–292.

McCord describes a number of gestures she says were used on the campus of the University of California, Berkeley. We do not know if they were common across the United States at that time, but several are not common now, for example, "Making the signs C or T with the forefinger or forefingers signifies a request for coffee or tea or an invitation to the taproom" and "Crossing the eyes signifies a comment on the person speaking. It may mean, 'I'm thinking just what you're thinking about him'; it may emphasize what he is saying; it may recall experience shared with the one to whom it is directed."

She describes and comments on "That's one for me (you)" (our *Scoring a point*): "The phrase 'Chalk one up,' or using the forefinger as an imaginary chalk to mark a board (the forefinger is occasionally dampened on the tongue at the start) is a recognition of a witty remark or pun. It is slightly less derogatory than the usual groans or sneers. It is perhaps derived from an English custom of chalking up on a wall the direct hits in a dart game."

---

[94] "¿Tú? ¿Usted? ¿Tú eres Pedro? ¿Usted es Pedro? Tienes que hacerlo tú."
[95] "Este es il jarrón nuevo," "Quiero esa muñeca."

MEISSNER, Martin and Stuart B. PHILPOTT, illustrated by Diana PHILPOTT
1975   A Dictionary of Sawmill Workers' Signs
       Sign Language Studies vol. 9, pp. 309- 347.

This is a dictionary of conventional gestures whose use is limited to sawmill workers. The abstract on p. 310 says:

> Their serendipitous discovery of an extensive lexicon of signs used by sawmill workers becomes even more significant with their evidence that signs of this kind—which have been called "emblems" and said to be used only in isolation —are in fact put into sentence-like utterances.

This sign system does not seem to be an independent system of communication like American gestures. Rather, it is closer to a system of signed English, enforced on the workers because of noise and distance in the mills. The signs do not signify any complex idea or emotional state that is not immediately translatable into English except for "Special signs with complex meanings" on pp. 315–316, which signify complete statements such as "Can't handle it" or "Log not tight against block" that are peculiar to the work in sawmills. Every other gesture means one or two distinct English words; for example, the symbol for "weak" (p. 342) is to hold the biceps of a relaxed arm, which is also used to mean "week." As such, it is easy to string gestures together to get a sentence, just as with the English words. For example, "It's time to change the blade" is conveyed by: (1) It's time = point to wrist as wristwatch, then (2) change = clenched fists crossed one over the other in front of body at waist level drawn past each other left to right so left hand ends on left side of body and similarly for right hand, then (3) blade = point to teeth. There are signs corresponding to particular verbs, which also allows for easy construction of statements.

MEO-ZILIO, Giovanni
1960   Consideraciones Generales sobre el Lenguaje de los Gestos
       Boletâin de Filologia (Universidade de Chile, Santiago de Chile), vol. XII, pp. 225–248.
1961   El Lenguaje de los Gestos en Uruguay
       Boletâin de Filologia (Universidade de Chile, Santiago de Chile), vol. XIII, pp. 75–163.

> Revised versions of these two papers appear in Meo-Zilio, 1989. They are collected as *El Lenguaje de los Gestos en el Río de la Plata*, Imp. Libertad, Montevideo, 1961, with the addition of a bibiliography and a few illustrations.

These two papers are meant as a single work. The first is the theoretical background and the second is a gestuary for Uruguay that also includes many new ideas based on the observations. Many of the ideas and distinctions Meo-Zilio makes are not found elsewhere and are apparently unknown to most researchers working since him. For this reason we include a longer description of this work. Unless noted otherwise, page numbers refer to the second paper.

Meo-Zilio describes his method of collecting gestures:

> I present, then, the material contained in this work, as fruit almost exclusively of observation and personal reflection.[96]

Meo-Zilio was native to Italy, and this work compared his experience with gestures there and in Uruguay:

> I will begin with an empirical distinction, for convenience, between those [gestures] that were unknown to me before arriving in Rio de la Plata and those that were familiar to me through having observed them also in Italy.[97]

He says in these papers that he produced this gestuary in the Department of Linguistics of the Faculty of Humanities and Sciences of Montevideo with the assistance of a number of people there.

Meo-Zilio describes the class of gestures he presents:

> This research has as its goal the description of gestures in the language of Uruguayans. In it, not every gesture, without restriction, will be an object of analysis, but only those that are comprehensible to all, although not being employed by all (*social gestures*).
> (Footnote: I use the term "language" in the larger sense, as *instrument for exchanging meanings*.)[98]

In his gestuary he describes over 200 gestures. He first presents representative gestures (see the quote by him on p. 46 above), beginning with representative-symbolic ones that he has observed only in Uruguay, followed by those he observed in Uruguay that he also knew from Italy. The latter are grouped by the main body part that is employed in them, with variations or ones similar in appearance grouped together as well as synonyms grouped somewhat together.[99]

Meo-Zilio then presents non-representative gestures, which he divides into three classes:

> The non-representative or contextual gestures can be subdivided into
> a) the expressive-appellative ones, b) the pragmatic ones, c) the deictic ones.[100]

---

[96] Presento, pues, el material contentido en este trabajo, como fruto casi exclusivamente de observación y reflexión personal. p. 76.

[97] "Empezaré por una distinción empírica, de comodidad, entre los que me eran desconocidos antes de llegar al Rio de la Plata y los que me eran familiares por haberlos observado también en Italia." p. 75. Meo-Zilio, 1990b is a more detailed listing and commentary on gestures common in Uruguay that come from Italy. Meo-Zilio, 1989 indicates that he received his Ph.D. from Padua in 1945 and starting in 1950 he taught in Montevideo.

[98] Esta investigación tiene por finalidad la descripción de los gestos en el lenguaje de los uruguayos. En ella no será, sin embargo, objeto de análisis, cualquier gesto, sino solamente aquellos que son comprensibles para todos, aunque no sean empleados por todos (*gestos sociales*). (Empleo el término "lenguaje" en sentido amplio, como *instrumento para intercambiar significados*.) p. 75.

[99] He adopts the term *isogestures* for what we have called "synonymous gestures".
"Adopto provisioriamente el término de *isogesto*; mas adelante, al llegar al capítulo sobre *sistema de oposiciones funcionales*, lo llamaré *isosquema*. Los isogestos tienen el mismo valor y función que tienen los sinónimos en la lengua. p. 103

[100] Los *no representativos* o *contextuales* pueden subdividirse en: a) *expresivo-apelativos*, b) *pragmáticos*, c) *deicticos*. p. 92

The gestures that he presents for (a) on pp. 151–156 seem to be mostly stylized emotions or illustrative gestures. The other non-representative gestures he describes on pp. 156–163 are greetings or are erotic.

On p. 133 he states, "A general principle: That the less abstract, less arbitrary, less *linguistic* [gestures] are common to distinct communities and vice-versa." However, the examples he gives are not common in the U.S. For example, we don't have a gesture for "let's eat," though it's likely that we would recognize the one he gives of grouping fingers in the shape of a pear and directing them to the mouth. The communities he is comparing are Italy and Uruguay, and he says that many Uruguayan gestures come from Italy via immigrants.

In the first paper he also says that women gesture more than men.

> Women, in relation to men, customarily express themselves, in general, with more affect, with less conceptual precision (and, in consequence, with greater quantity of verbal material); from this derives (fundamentally) the necessity to recur more fully to the auxiliary language of gestures.[101]

This contradicts Morris, 1994.

In the first paper, pp. 238–245, he compares the language of gestures to the language of the deaf and reviews the literature about the syntax of gestures.

At the end of his work, Meo-Zilio presents what he calls a "system of functional oppositions" for gestures, which he says are similar to ones for verbal language.[102] In the summary in Section 8 of the second paper, p. 150, he lists the following oppositions, for which he gives many examples:

---

[101]   Las mujeres, en relación con los hombres, suelen expresarse, en general, con más afectividad, con menos precisión conceptual (y, por consiguiente, con más cantidad de material verbal); en ello deriva (fundamentalmente) la necesidad de recurrir más ampliamente al lenguaje auxiliar de los gestos. p. 227.

[102]   *También en los gestos aparece (mutatis mutandis) el "sistema de oposiciones funcionales" que ya se aplica corrientemente en el estudio de lenguaje fónico.* En efecto, la relativa escasez de los gestos disponibles (del mismo modo que lo limitado de los sonidos en la lengua) ha determinado en ellos el surgir de elementos funcionales diferenciadores de su significación. Así, por ej., entre los gestos indicadores de *gran cantidad/¿qué quieres?* el factor *amplitud del movimiento* es el elemento diferenciador (*rasgo pertinente*); en la oposición de los gestos *indicadores de "gran cantidad"/"miedo"*, el rasgo pertinente es la *presencia/ausencia* del *movimiento* de abertura-cerrazón. Así mismo, en las oposición *escaparse/escápese* el factor *presencia/ausencia de expresión verbal* concomitante puede determinar el valor de *imperativo/no imperativo*; en el mismo orden de gestos, el factor *presencia/ausencia del sonido extrafónico* correspondiente (chasquido) determina otra distinción semántica: *escaparse/fino (/untuoso)*. El último orden de gestos indica que son posibles, en este campo, *oposiciones funcionales múltiples* sobre la base física del mismo ademán (*paradigma*): en este caso, existen por lo menos tres oposiciones, una entre el gesto solo y el gesto acompañado por expresiones verbales, otra entre el gesto puro y el gesto acompañado por el sonido estrafónico correspondiente, y otra más entre el gesto puro con movimiento frotamiento y el mismo con movimiento de *contacto/no contacto*. p. 117

Static / Dynamic
Wide [large, ample] / Not wide
Rapid / Slow
Prolonged / Brief
High / Low
High / Very high
Tense / Loose
Simple / Iterated
Monolateral / Bilateral
With verbal expression / Without verbal expression
Movement out / Movement out and back
With movement of opening / Without movement of opening
With extralinguistic sound / Without extralinguistic sound
With extraphonic sound / Without extraphonic sound
Vertical movement / Non-vertical movement
Downwards / Upwards
Vertical plane / Horizontal plane
With physical concomitant / Without physical concomitant
Context *x* / Context *y*

He takes these oppositions to amount to something like phonemes (p. 144).

MEO-ZILIO, Giovanni
1989 *Estudos Hispanoamericanos: Temas Lingüísticos*
     Bulzoni Editore.

Chapter 7 of this is about gestures generally and Hispanic American gestures particularly. It is drawn from Meo-Zilio's other work. Section 7.2 is "Some Uruguayan gestures" drawn from Meo-Zilio, 1961, in which he discusses some of the gestures investigated in that earlier work.

   In Section 7.3.3 he points out that in some Hispanic American countries there are gestural markers for singular and plural.

MEO-ZILIO, Giovanni
1990a Gestos Eróticos en el Dominio Hispánico
     In *Les Langues Néo-Latines*, Paris, no. 274, fascicule 3, pp. 83-98.

This is a list of 91 gestures or variants that "can be considered erotic in the sense that they represent or refer to the [sexual] organs or erotic-sexual activity."[103] It is a list only, supplementing Meo-Zilio and Mejía, 1980–1983. But here for each gesture only one country is given as an example of where the gesture is common, and the gestures are described only verbally.

   The gestures are classified according in the following categories:

---

[103] . . . pueden considerarse eróticos en el sentido de que representan o aluden a los órganos o a la actividad erótico-sexual. p. 83

Gestures that represent, indicate or refer to the masculine sexual organs:
> Phallic gestures with icastic significance ("valor") (imitative of form, size, quality, or state);
> Phallic gestures with meaning ("valor") of an "insult";
> Gestures that represent or refer to the testicles;
> Gestures that represent or refer to the complete male organ with the meaning ("valor") of an insult

Gestures that represent or refer to the feminine sexual organs or their qualities:
Gestures with icastic significance ("valor") (imitative of form, size, or quality);
> Gestures with meaning ("valor") of an insult and bad omen ("agüero").[104]

MEO-ZILIO, Giovanni and J. COSNIER
1987 Expresiones 'Linguísticas' Concomitantes con Expresiones Gestuales em España e Hispanoamerica
Diálogos Hispánicos de Amsterdam, vol. 6, pp. 65-79.

This is an study of some sounds produced vocally that are not words that are accompany gestures. For example, the authors say that in Colombia the sound "¡AJ!" is made while holding a closed hand to your forehead, the entire complex of gesture and sound meaning "hangover, indisposition following a drunken spree" (*resaca, malestar que sigue a una borrachera*). Each of the sounds is keyed to one or more gestures from Meo-Zilio and Mejía 1980–1983 (annotated below), and an indication is given for which country the gesture and sound complex is made. Entries that have sounds that can be written are alphabetized, while those that are described only by how the mouth and vocal apparatus are used are in a separate section. There are about 80 entries, some sounds having multiple gestures associated with them. See the discussion of similar sounds used with American gestures in Section III.A above, especially footnote 24.

MEO-ZILIO, Giovanni and Silvia MEJÍA
1980- *Diccionário de Gestos: España e Hispanoamérica*
1983   Vol. I, 1980, and Vol. II, 1983. Instituto Caro y Cuervo Yerbabuena, Bogotá, Colombia.

This two volume set constitutes a dictionary of gestures for Spain and Spanish-speaking countries of the Americas. Meo-Zilio and Mejía list over 2,000 gestures, all of which are described verbally and many of which are illustrated with photographs, some of which are marked to indicate movement. Each gesture entry lists the countries in which it is common.

---

[104] Gestos que representan, indican o aluden a los órganos sexuales maculinos:
> Gestos que representam o aluden al phallus
>> Gestos fálicos con valor icástico (imitativos de forma, tamaño, cualidad o estado)
>> Gestos fálicos con valor de "insulto"
> Gestos que representan o aluden a los testiculos
> Gestos que representan o aluden al órgano sexual masculino completo con valor de "insulto"
Gestos que representan o aluden al órgano sexual feminino o a sus cualidades
> Gestos con valor icástico (imitativos de su forma, tamaño o cualidad
> Gestos con valor de insulto y mal agüero

Meo-Zilio and Mejía describe the class of gestures by referring to Meo-Zilio 1960, 1961 for terminology:

> ... *representative* gestures (symbolic and icastic) and *contextual* gestures (expressive-appellative, pragmatic, and indicative) ... Excluded, in general, are those gestures that are merely imitative of basic actions of practical daily life (that are, more or less, the same everywhere)—except special cases for their metaphoric value or for the richness or the complexity of their variants—and those merely mechanical or reflexive ones whose interest is more for physiology or psychology than the science of communication.[105]

They describe their method of collecting gestures:

> For methodological and practical motives that linguists know well, we have used essentially for each country, a single report whose results, in case of doubt, were controlled *in loco* by other informants. For Mexico and Peru the research has been repeated a second time because it could not be completed the first time by the same informant.[106]

They list one informant from each of Argentina, Bolivia, Colombia, Costa Rica, Cuba, Chile, Ecuador, Spain, Guatemala, Honduras, Mexico, Nicaragua, Panama, Paraguay, Peru, Salvador, Venezuela, and Uruguay, giving the birthplace of each in that country. In the second volume they add informants and gestures from Puerto Rico and the Dominican Republic. They speak of a questionnaire that the informants used to begin their collections (Vol. I, p. 9), but they do not reproduce it.

About the entries they say:

> It is clear that our attempt does not pretend to exhaust (nor could it objectively) the wide field of gestural language, which in large part is still unexplored, within the selected communities, but *to bring together in a systematic detailed manner a first provisional list of gestures ordered according to their basic meaning*, and accompanied by *morphological* and semantic descriptions (with their variants).
>
> In cases where the description of the gesture is difficult to represent mentally for the non-specialist reader, we have adjoined corresponding photographs. The same has been done with those gestures for which the facial expression is especially important (especially because these last are difficult to describe objectively in their analytic components).

---

[105] ... gestos *representativos* (simbólicos e icásticos) y *contextuales* (expresivo-apelativos, pragmatícos e indicativos) ... Se excluyen, por lo general, los gestos meramente imitativos de acciones elementales de la vida práctica (que son más o menos iguales en todas partes)—salvo casos especiales por su valor metafórico o por la riqueza o la complejidad de sus variantes—y los meramente mecánicos o reflejos que interesan a la fisiología o la sociología más que a las ciencias de la comunicación. Vol. 1, p. 7.

[106] Por los motivos metodológicos y prácticos que los lingüistas bien conocen, se ha utilizado fundamentalmente, para cada país, un solo informe cuyas resultancias, en casos de dudas, se han controloado *in loco* con otros informantes. Para México y Perú la encuesta ha tenido que repetirse una segunda vez por no haber podido completarse la primera con el mismo informante. Vol. I, p. 8.

We have completed the description of certain gestures with the corresponding linguistic expressions, but only in those cases which were suggested
spontaneously by our informants to effect (or to recognize) the gesture.[107]

They say that an appendix with theoretical considerations will appear in a later
volume, apparently one on Luso-Brazilian gestures, but it seems that was never
published.

They do not make explicit why they have grouped Spanish-speaking countries
together for these two volumes nor why they plan another volume for Brazil and
Portugal.[108]

MITTON, A.
1949   La Langage par Gestes
       Nouvelle Revue des Traditions Populaire, vol. 1, pp. 138–151.

The author lists 79 French gestures along with some variations. Each entry has three
parts: (i) definition of the gesture, in which the movement is described verbally;
(ii) its meaning, in which various ways are used to describe the meaning: a verbal
phrase (in French), a description of its role (#2, "Interrogation," along with two
phrases), or an emotion or affect (#5, "Hate. Serious threat.", #9, "Friendship"); and
(iii) observations, which can include comments about whether the gesture is familiar,
whether it is a "schematization of a natural gesture," and etymologies, including
psychological analyses.

---

[107] Claro que está que esta nuestra tentativa no pretende agotar (ni lo podría objetivamente) el
dilatado campo del lenguaje gestual, en gran parte todavía sin explorar, dentro de las comunidades
elegidas, sino *reunir de manera sistemática y detallada una primera lista provisional de gestos
ordenados según su significado* fundamental y acompañados de la descripción *morfológica* y
semántica (con sus variantes).

En los casos en que la descripción del gesto es difícil de representarse mentalmente por un
lector no especialista, se han agregado las fotografías correspondientes. Lo mismo se ha hecho con
los gestos para los cuales es especialmente importante la mímica facial (justamente por ser, esta
última, difícil de describir objetivamente en sus componentes analíticos).

Hemos completado la descripción de ciertos gestos con las expresiones lingüísticas
correspondientes, pero sólo en los casos en que hayan surgido espontáneamente en nuestros
informantes el efectuar (o al reconocer) el gesto. Vol. 1, p. 8.

[108] Antoni Turull, 1983, suggests:

Circumscribing this dictionary of gestures to Spain and Hispano-America has an obvious
reason. Although some gestures coincide in places with distinct idioms, there is a
greater gestural unity in places of similar speech.

El hecho de que este diccionario de gestos esté circunscrito a España e Hispanoamérica
tiene una razón obvia. Si bien algunos gestos coninciden en lugares de idiomas
distintos, hay una mayor unidad gestual en los lugares de habla similar. p. 630.

Meo-Zilio 1960–1961 more naturally compares Uruguayan gestures with Italian gestures, since
a large part of the population in Uruguay is descended from Italians. It would seem at least as important to compare Brazilian gestures to those from Africa, whose cultural influences are as central in
Brazil as those from Portugal.

The collection seems to be comprised mostly of conventional gestures, some stylized emotions, and at least one speech marker (#77).

There is no explanation of how the author collected and noted the meaning of these gestures, though the text makes it appear that he is a native speaker of them.

Mitton suggests categories for gestures, giving at least one example of each:

As one distinguishes in language various "parts of discourse"—substantives, verbs, exclamations, etc.—one could distinguish in gestures various categories (although these categories are more fluid than those of our grammar):

Imperative gestures
Enunciative gestures
Substantive gestures
Interrogative gestures
Negative gestures
Numeral gestures
Demonstrative gestures
Personal pronouns
Exclamatory or emotive gestures
Expletive gestures[109]

He says that French gestures distinguish between cardinal (#55) and ordinal numbers (#56).[110]

Mitton says that via the use of pronouns it is possible to conjugate verbs and create assertions with sequential combinations of gestures. The examples he gives on p. 140 are (with the number of the gestures in parentheses):

"I am not thirsty" ("Je n'ai pas soif") = Me (20) To be thirsty (51) Not (3).

"Is he hungry?" ("A-t-il faim?") = Is it that (2) He (22) To be hungry (52).

These are in the present tense; compare the annotation for Calbris, 1990.

MONAHAN, Barbara
1983 *A Dictionary of Russian Gesture*
Hermitage, Ann Arbor, Michigan.

This is a listing of about 80 gestures. Each is illustrated with a photograph; movement is sometimes indicated by photos of successive parts of the gesture. Sometimes a comment about the context for a gesture is included, and in two cases there are pictures of gestures done in context (two women talking and walking, p. 79 and p. 81). Monahan notes when a gesture is used only by men, only by women, or both.

---

[109] De même qu'on distingue dan le langage diverses "parties du discours"—substantives, verbs, exclamations, etc.—on pourrait distinguer dan les gestes diverse catégories (toutefois ces catégories sont plus floues que celles de nos grammaires). pp. 139–140.

[110] p. 48 #55. Saisir successivement, dans la poigne droigt, le pouce, l'index et le majeur de la main gauche. "Primo, secundo, tertio." #56, "Les deux mains à hauteur du visage, paume en avant, les doigts repliés,

montrer le pouce droit . . . = un.
— le pouce et l'index droits . . . = deux. . . .

Most of the gestures she illustrates are conventional, with some stylized emotions (p. 28–29, "To grab one's head in frustration"), plus entries on how people walk or talk together ("Women conversing" p. 78, "Women walking arm in arm" p. 80). Eleven are sexual.

The organization of the entries is by the following categories:

1. Confusion, Perplexity, Frustration
2. Drinking
3. Mockery and Self-Mockery
4. Personal Contact
5. Warning Gestures
6. Expressions of Personal Needs and Desires
7. Superstition
8. Sexual Gestures
9. Approval and Disapproval
10. Miscellaneous

Monahan does not make clear whether it is Russia she is talking about or the Soviet Union. She says that one of her informants is from the Ukraine, and in several places says whether a gesture is common in the Ukraine but not in Russia. But there's no comment about other republics in the USSR.

> If one can accept, for the moment, the idea of a National character, without being seduced by the myth of the "Russian soul," one may generalize that the Russian national is typically more expansive and demonstrative than his comparatively reticent American counterpart. This is certainly true if the language of gesture is a suitable indicator.
>
> ... I feel I can state with some assurance that the role of gesticulation in Russian life is of much greater variety and significance than it is in our own culture. p. 13

She does not say what she means by "expansive" and "demonstrative."

MORRIS, Desmond
1977 *Manwatching: A Field Guide to Human Behavior*
    Harry N. Abrams, Inc.

In this book about a wide range of non-verbal communication, Morris discusses many conventional gestures. Most are illustrated. Morris does not say how he knows the gestures he discusses except for those that are in Morris, Collett, Marsh, and O'Shaughnessy, 1979, which was apparently written prior to this work since Morris draws on it in a number of places and cites it in his bibliography.

MORRIS, Desmond
1994 *Bodytalk: The Meaning of Human Gestures*
    Crown Trade Paperbacks.

This is a collection of over 600 movements and postures from around the world. "To make it easier to find your way around this guide, each gesture has been classified by its major body part." No cross-referencing is given for gestures of the same or similar meaning.

Each entry consists of:

- A name in terms of the major body part involved.
- A drawing without indication of movement.
- The meaning.
- A description of the movement.
- The background, elaborating on the meaning in terms of context or etymology.
- The locations where the gesture is common.

No indication is given of how the gestures were collected. No discussion is given for what criteria were used for deciding what was to be included or excluded. In the mix are conventional gestures, ritual gestures, stylized emotions, and some quite bizarre entries. For example, on p. 41 "Ear nibble" is given, which is said to mean "I love you," yet in the background part of the entry Morris more correctly identifies this as sexual foreplay. We are curious why sexual intercourse is not then shown as meaning "I love you a lot" as we were taught in high school. Morris also includes a number of gestures that he says are unconscious, for example, "Body lean" on p. 11 for "I am paying attention." But he includes so few of these relative to the immense number of physical clues from which inferences can be made that we have no idea on what basis the selection was made. Morris says in the preface:

> Gender Note: Anyone noticing that most of the sketches depict males might come to the conclusion that this shows an unfair gender bias. This is not the case. It is not this book that is sexist, it is the gestures themselves. For some reason, signalling by gesture is a predominantly masculine pursuit. In some countries it is so exclusively masculine that our female researchers had to withdraw before the local men would even discuss the subject.

Other research on gender and gesture contradicts this (Poling, 1978, Meo-Zilio, 1960, both annotated above).

A number of entries have parts that are wrong. For example, "Belly rub" (p. 10) is said to mean hunger and is listed as worldwide, but it is not used in the U.S. "Elbow flap" (p. 49), where the elbows are raised and lowered rhythmically while the gesturer makes a clucking noise like a hen, is said by Morris to mean "You are a coward" and is listed as only in North America, but no one we know in North America knows it. For one gesture, the "Ear Pull" (p. 41), Morris gives as location "Jewish communities," apparently unaware that there are three quite different Jewish communities with very different cultures and gestures: Ashkenazi (from Eastern Europe), Sephardic (from Spain and Muslim countries), and Israeli, as well as Jewish communities that are fully acculturated to another culture (compare Efron, 1941/1972). This particular gesture is unknown in acculturated Jewish communities in the U.S.

In sum, we have no reason to believe that the entries are accurate.

MORRIS, Desmond, Peter COLLET, Peter MARSH, and Marie O'SHAUGHNESSY
1979 *Gestures: Their Origins and Distribution*
   Jonathan Cape.

The authors choose 20 physical movements that were determined to be symbolic in at least some part of Western Europe.

> At each of the 40 locations [in Western Europe], 30 adult male subjects were selected at random in public places, such as streets, squares, parks, bars, quaysides, or restaurants, and were shown a sheet of standard drawings depicting the 20 key gestures. . . .
>   We restricted ourselves to male informants because it was known that in some areas women would be reluctant to co-operate, especially where "taboo" insult gestures were concerned. In general, very old and very young informants were also avoided. A typical informant could be characterized as a middle-aged male in the middle- or lower-income bracket, who was relaxing in some public place, with a little time to spare. In general, our informants were immensely helpful and patient, and responded seriously and thoughtfully to our queries. If we ignored the more sophisticated and better educated of the males who were available it was simply because we feared that they might be too well travelled and know too much about gestures foreign to their particular locality. There was always a danger that, in such cases, they would wish to show off their knowledge, and in so doing would slightly distort the true, local picture. pp. xiii–xiv

They then chart the various meanings ascribed to the movements according to their regional distribution. The authors do not reproduce the protocol of their interviews. Drawings of the gestures are reproduced in the book, though it is not made clear whether these were the ones shown to the subjects.
   A basic point of their research is the following:

> Many of the gestures extended their ranges across national and linguistic boundaries. Remarkably few of the gestures we studied could be labelled as exclusively British, French, Italian, or as belonging to some other specific country. This discovery contradicts a great deal of what has been written in the past about so called "national gestures". There are, however, a number of gesture *meanings* which are truly national in their territorial restriction.

Thus, the authors identify a gesture as a particular symbolic physical action, independent of what meaning may be attached to it. Given one particular symbolic movement, the authors treat it as a single gesture that has evolved its meaning as it was adopted in various areas, looking always for an *ur*-gesture. But no reason is given for why the same physical movement could not have come to be used independently in different areas with different associated meanings. Literary evidence of the history of a gesture is often used to good effect, but citing paintings from antiquity that show the same physical movement is not useful: without knowing the meaning of the physical movement or even whether that movement was symbolic at that time, there is no reason to think that the movement depicted has any relation to the modern gesture. The same movement has often come to have radically different meanings in different cultures, and within a culture a symbolic movement can change its meaning rapidly.[111] Moreover, some gestures fall out of use,[112] and there is no reason to think that the same movement could not be used at some later time, perhaps even centuries later, with a completely different meaning.

The result is some very fanciful etymologies, which start as conjectures and quickly harden into assertions. Consider, for example, the hand purse ("The fingers and thumb of one hand are straightened and brought together in a point facing upwards"). The authors begin by focusing on its significance as indicating precision or a query that the other speaker be more precise. We suspect that the latter is distinguished from the former by facial movements. But the authors did not take into account facial expression in studying gestures, and, as Adam Kendon, 1992, says,

> As Ricci-Bitti et al. point out, it is doubtless because facial expression
> was omitted altogether by Morris et al., in their study of patterns of use of
> conventional gestures in different locations in Europe, that their results are,
> in some cases, so puzzling.[113]

The authors then say about the hand purse:

> A totally different meaning has arisen elsewhere. From the basic statement
> of precise emphasis, the message has been transformed into "this thing has
> precision". From there it has changed to "this has class", to "high quality",
> to "excellent", to "good". So although the hand purse may be a query, often
> an irritable one, in one region, it can also be a satisfied or excited signal of
> excellence in another. p. 46

Nowhere do they cite any references to show that this transformation is anything more than their imaginative reconstruction of what might have happened. After citing more meanings for this movement, they say:

> Those, then, are the six major meanings for the hand purse gesture that we have
> encountered in the field. Had we travelled beyond the European-Mediterranean zone,
> we might have discovered even more. It is clearly a multi-message gesture with a
> complex cultural history of local specialization and differentiation. p. 55

Compare: We go to various countries with a list of "words" and find that the sound "kon" (pronounced with a long "o") is recognized in Spain and Portugal and England, though with a different meaning in the first two countries from the latter. We say we have the same "word" with different meanings, and then we go looking for the *ur*-word behind them both. What is the basic message that somehow got transformed into meaning "with" in Spain and Portugal and "a solid with circle for its base and a curved surface tapering evenly to an apex" in English? Should we say

---

[111] See the discussion of the "V" sign on p. 51 above.

[112] For example, the *mano cornuta* in the U.S. discussed on p. 50 above.

[113] Ricci Bitti, Boggi-Cavallo, Brighetti, and Garotti, 1987, pp. 171–178. See also Ricci Bitti and Poggi, 1991, pp. 450–451.

that this is a multi-message word with "a complex cultural history of local speciali-
zation and differentiation"? The authors do not ask themselves if the assumptions
they make are sensible for the study of communication.[114]

MORSBACH, Helmut
1973 Aspects of Nonverbal Communication in Japan
  The Journal of Nervous and Mental Disease, vol. 157, pp. 262–277.

Included in a general discussion of Japanese non-verbal behavior are descriptions of
16 conventional gestures. Though not made explicit, the text suggests that the author
lived in Japan and spoke Japanese. See the quote from this article on p. 23 above
(footnote 25).

MORSBACH, Helmut
1988 Nonverbal Communication and Hierarchical Relationships: The Case of Bowing in Japan
  In *Cross-Cultural Perspectives in Nonverbal Communication*, ed. Fernando Poyatos,
  C. J. Hogrefe, pp. 189–199.

The article contains information about a number of different kinds and contexts of
bowing in Japan, though the movements of those are not clearly described.

MUNARI, Bruno
1963 *Supplemento al Dizionario Italiano*
  Muggiani Editore Milano. Reprinted 2002 Corriani Editore.
  Reprinted with only the Italian and English as *Speak Italian: The Fine Art of the Gesture—*
  A Supplement to the Italian Dictionary, Chronicle Books, 2005.

This is a collection of 49 conventional gestures presented as a supplement to an
Italian dictionary and as an aid to foreigners visiting Italy. It is not clear whether
these gestures are common to all of Italy or only Naples.

  The gestures are illustrated with photographs along with verbal descriptions of
movement (the descriptions on p. 94 and p. 104 are reversed). The text is in Italian,
French, English, and German. There is no discussion of the context of use for most
of the gestures. The author does not tell us how he came to choose these gestures
other than to say that he excluded those that were obscene or vulgar.

---

[114] Compare Joseph H. Greenberg, *Essays in Linguistics*, 1957:

  It is clear that, in principle, the connection between sound and meaning is arbitrary, in the
  sense that any meaning can be represented by any combination of sounds. A dog may as
  easily be called *Hund, cane, sabaka,* or *kalb* and, in fact, is—in German, Italian, Russian,
  and Arabic, respectively. Moreover, the thousands of meaningful forms of any language
  are basically independent. . . . From these two principles of the arbitrariness of the sound-
  meaning connection and the independence of meaningful forms, it follows that resemblances
  beyond chance in both form and meaning require a historical explanation, whether through
  borrowing or through common origin. . . . On the other hand, similarity in meaning not
  accompanied in sound or similarity in sound without corresponding similarity in meaning
  may be considered of negligible value. pp. 35–36

NISSET, Luc
2007 *French in Your Face!*
    McGraw-Hill.

This is a textbook for American students learning French. It contains a section with 44 gestures divided into sections: Annoyance (4), Food and drink (4), Insults (8), Praise, promises, denial (4), The senses (4), Talk (8), Time and money (4), Transportation (4), Miscellaneous (4). Each gesture is illustrated by the author with a cartoon showing the face and as much of the body as necessary to illustrate the movement. No further explanation of how to do the movement is given. Each cartoon has a number of bubbles containing French phrases, with very free English translations below the cartoon. The phrases and translations seem to be what could be said with the gesture. For example, for the gesture where a man strikes the inside of his arm above the elbow with the palm of his other hand, and the forearm is raised in concert with that, the phrases are: "Go to hell!" "Up yours!" "With all the taxes we pay, the hell with it!" "Fuck you!" We are not told whether the author is a native speaker of French or how he knows these gestures.

OLIVERI, Fabio, illustrations by Jasmin CARNABUCI
2000 *La Gestualità dei Siciliani*
    2nd edition, KREA.

This is a collection of Sicilian conventional gestures, the introduction of which is in Italian and English. The author says:

> In the history of Sicilian culture [this] is the first attempt to draw up a map of the most representative aspects of the Sicilian use of gestures. p. 20

There are 79 entries. Presented first are ones that use only one hand, then ones that use two hands, and then ones that use hands and parts of the body. No index or table of contents is given.

Each entry begins with an illustration of the principal part of the body involved in the movement. If the face is shown, it is only to place the movement relative to it, and a neutral expression is shown. In some drawings dotted lines and arrows are used to indicate movement.

Below the illustration there is a title in Sicilian. In some cases this is the meaning ("Essiri tiratu," "to be stingy," p. 140) and in others it is a phrase that accompanies the gesture ("Cu' licca nun sicca," "Those who lick do not dry up," pp. 130–131). Then an explanation is given in Italian, English, French, German, and Japanese of the meaning of the gesture. Some are quotations from volume 2 of Pitré, 1889 (annotated below) that the author says served as a source for much of the book.

Of special interest is a movement that has different meanings when done by the left hand versus the right:

> The person selling fruit and vegetables, fish or services, when he gets his first takings in the morning, as a way of making the rest of the working day go well,

makes the sign of the cross with his right hand. Having made the sign of the cross or not means having already earned something or otherwise. But in this case the sign is made with the right hand. Instead, making it with the left hand expresses amazement, wonder, consternation. Faced with an incredible, dramatic event which has already occurred or may occur, people at once have recourse to the arcane gesture of making the sign of the cross with the left hand. pp. 18–19

PAPPAS, William
1972 *Instant Greek*
Erminoni Argolis, Greece. 12th edition published in 1999 by Chetwynd Stapylton, USA.

The author is a South African of Greek descent who spent twelve years in Greece, mainly in a small fishing village. He thanks 30 people who helped him with the collection.

The book has entries for 69 gestures. Each has a title which is a phrase that is a verbal equivalent of the movement. A verbal description is given of the movement, and additional information about context and meaning is added. On the facing page a cartoon, drawn by the author, illustrates the use of the gesture. Each cartoon is of the same character, an older man, showing the entire body and face.

Though some of the entries are clearly conventional gestures, some appear to be illustrative gestures (pantomimes):

"Chicken"
Flap your arms energetically and if you like let out the odd crow. p. 62

"By aeroplane?" [enlarging the question "How did you come here?"]
Outstretch your arms and wheel about above your head. p. 46

Of particular interest are:

"No," pp. 64–65, which is to tilt the head back as in our *Come here–head*.
"Yes," pp. 96–97, which is the same movement as our *Nod of the head–acknowledgement*.
"Before–many years ago," pp. 28–29, waving the open palm, fingers up, backwards toward your shoulder, which suggests that it is possible to speak of the past using Greek gestures.

PAURA, Bruno and Marina SORGE, drawings by Alessia CIANFLONE
1999 *Comme te l'Aggia Dicere? Ouvere L'arte Gestuale a Napoli*
The Art of Gestures in Naples—L'Art des Gestes à Naples—El Arte de los Gestos en Nápoles
Edizioni Intra Moenia.

Though the title is given in four languages, the only parts of the book that are not in Italian are the translations of the gesture into a word or phrase. The English translations are sometimes odd (e.g., "mingy" for "stingy," "What a luck!").

Some of the entries are illustrated with a drawing that shows the face as well as the position of the hand or part of the body. Others are illustrated with photographs.

Some of the drawings show movement; none of the photographs do. Some photographs have serious distractions that affect our ability to see the gesture, as in the photo for number 72, *Te ceco ll'uocchie!*, which is translated as "I blind you!" and has a woman with a smiling look.

There are 111 entries for what appear to be conventional gestures. They are initially presented in sections that are labeled by a kind of meaning ("To drink" (*Bere*), "Tomorrow" (*Domani*), or the kind of speech act, "To ask, requests" (*Chiedere, Chiedersi*). An index of the gestures with those divisions is given at the end of the book. Following that there is a "Guide to the identification of the gestures" that lists the gestures according to the shape of the hand and, if that is not relevant, then under the classifications "Fingers extended" (*Dita distese*) or "Arms outstretched" (*Braccia allargate*).

Each entry has the following parts: (i) a heading for one or more gestures, for example, "Go slowly" (*Andare piano*); "To appreciate, to praise" (*Aprezzare, Elogiare*); (ii) a number of the gesture; (iii) a title of the gesture, which seems to be words that are or can be spoken with the gesture; (iv) a translation into Italian, English, French, and Spanish, which is sometimes but not always the phrase that is the title; (v) a description of how to make the gesture; (vi) a further description of how to use the gesture in context.

Gesture Number 33 is *Dimmane; Aroppo* translated as "Tomorrow; After." It is not the same as described by Szarota, 2008 (annotated below).

PAYRATÓ, Lluis
1989   Assaig de Dialectologia Gestual: Aproximació Pragmàtica al Repetori Bàsic d'Emblemes del Català de Barcelona
       Ph.D. Thesis, University of Barcelona
1993   A Pragmatic View on Autonomous Gestures: A First Repertoire of Catalan Emblems
       Journal of Pragmatics, vol. 20, pp. 193–216.

The second of these is a summary and report on the first, with a survey of the literature and a discussion of the evolution of gestures. All quotations below are from that article.

Payrató's goal is to develop a basic repertory of Catalan emblems. Here is how on pp. 195–197 he characterizes the gestures he is studying:

> The emblem was defined in the present research in the following way: as an (a) *autonomous gesture*, i.e. a gestural act which can take place independently of the verbal language, (b) made with a full communicative intention, (c) typical of a human community, and (d) with a significative nucleus or semantic core which makes possible an easy and brief translation to a natural language and an unequivocal recognition by members of the speech community where the gesture is used. This definition represents an attempt to harmonize previous proposals and to make concrete and stress some characteristics of emblematic gestures:
>
> *(1) Autonomy from speech*. An emblem can be displayed unaccompanied by verbal material . . .

    (2) Communicative goal. The emblem is an autonomous gesture that is deliberatively informative, that is to say, *communicative.* An interlocutor, by means of an emblem, intentionally sends a message to the other interlocutor(s). By intentionality it is meant that, in contrast, for instance, with what happens when one displays affects, the sender is totally conscious of and responsible for the message, while the receiver(s) assume(s) that the action was done deliberately by the sender with the aim of conveying information.

    (3) Illocutionary force. The emblem is a communicative act that can be *reproduced by means of an illocutionary verbal act,* without altering the essence, the intention, and the perlocutive results of the action. What this really means is that emblems can always have illocutionary force, i.e. a power that in gestural tools is perfectly equivalent to illocutionary force. For this reason, the suitable communicative translation of an emblem can never be only a word or a sentence at its locutionary level, but has to include an illocutionary utterance.

    (4) Semantic core. From the viewpoint of the semantic content, an emblem can be associated in abstract with a significant nucleus or semantic core. This can be expressed with one or several words, which must be understood as *watchwords* or *keywords.* Some semantic details of the content and the overall sense of the action are not achieved outside real contexts of use, where concrete pragmatic interpretations are made and illocutionary values conferred.

    (5) Social nature. The semantic content and illocutionary value of the emblems are known by members of a given social group, for which the utilization of the emblems is unambiguous and their recognition immediate.[115]

Payrató's requirement that each gesture be translated into "natural language," which is part of the standard notion of emblem, seems to restrict attention to a smaller class of gestures than conventional. But the idea of the nucleus or semantic core of a gesture is unclear. In the entries in his list of gestures we see:

To go away ("Get out!", "Let's go!")
Approximately (Doubt, Ignorance)
To drink
Drunk (Drunkenness)
Taunt (Thumb out)
Keys (To open)
Request
To smoke
A lot (full)
Negation

He also calls these "keywords," and this looks like the idea of the message of a gesture, which we noted above has problems. There is no reason to think that because we can associate a word or phrase like the ones above to each gesture that there is an "easy and brief translation to a natural language" of the gesture. Further, the condition in item (d) that there must be "an unequivocal recognition by members

---

[115] See our discussion on p. 1 above of the difficulty of using the criterion of intentionality.

of the speech community where the gesture is used" is unclear: recognition of what? We consider this more in the comments below. In sum, it may well be that he is investigating Catalan conventional gestures.

Here is a description of his methodology:

(i) A provisional repertoire of 297 gestures which could be considered emblems (by Catalan speakers) was established. The criteria for classifying a gesture as an emblem were the five characteristics noted above. Previously, direct observation and bibliographical sources, mainly covering Catalan and Spanish gestures, had supplied a former set of 315 items that constituted the initial sample.

(ii) The use of the items mentioned was checked through a codification test applied to 10 informants with homogeneous traits: middle class men between 25 and 40 years old, born in Barcelona (as were their parents), speakers of Catalan as a first language, and educated (at least) to the high school level. In the test, informants were asked to perform gestural actions from simulated contexts, known from everyday life. A hundred and sixty contexts were prepared to elicit the gestures of the provisional repertoire. After each context had been read by the interviewer, all the performed actions were transcribed into the questionnaire, together with the informants' comments. Once the results were collected and analyzed, a few new gestures (made by the informants) were added to the first repertoire; the rest, including all those not performed by the informants or not clearly attested in the bibliographical sources, were eliminated. This first test also allowed the selection of more frequent morphological variants of many gestures, which were adopted as principal. The final result of this phase was called the *provisional basic repertoire (PBR)* of Catalan gestures, composed of 221 gestures.

(iii) The emblematic nature of the gestures of the *PBR* was checked by a second test applied to a new group of ten people (with the same characteristics as the former group). Informants were now asked to identify the preceding 221 gestures, reproduced in designs, photographs, and, when necessary, by the action of the interviewer himself. The results were tabulated and a (definitive) basic repertoire (*BR*) of 108 emblems used by Catalan speakers was set up.

Besides gestures excluded from the initial selection for not fulfilling the adopted criteria, two series of gestures which might be taken to be emblems were also rejected for different reasons. On the one hand, greetings, deictic gestures, and general measuring gestures were excluded, because we felt that their analysis needed a different methodology. On the other hand, gestures were rejected which were thought to be peculiar to certain groups of speakers, or to specific activities, such as those performed (only) in certain games, sports, professions, and so on. Such items are not included in what was supposed to make up the basic gestural repertoire associated with a language. 199–200

The list of 315 items that constituted the original sample appears in his thesis. The simulated contexts for (ii), which were presented verbally, are given in his thesis. We are not told exactly what the interviewers showed to the informants for the decoding test. In particular, some of the gestures have illustrations of women doing them, but we don't know if any of the people showing the gestures to the informants were women. However, the thesis does show that the informant was expected to write down what he thought the gesture meant on a single line—again, stressing the idea that each gesture was supposed to have a meaning that could easily be translated into ordinary language. We are not given the responses the informants made so we can't evaluate how Payrató made his judgments about whether they understood the gesture: what counts as getting the right meaning? We wonder whether the informant had to get the exact phrase that was previously associated with the gesture. This is important because it could be that the way he eliminated gestures was if they did not have an easy translation into natural language, though they might have had clear meaning to every single informant. Further, it is not clear whether the gestures were performed for the informants in context. If they were not performed in context, that could account for ambiguity. If they were performed in context, then some gestures that might not be known could be guessed at by the informants to give a higher reading for decoding. In sum, from what he presents here, his procedure is not reproducible, and we are at a loss how to evaluate what he did.

Here is how he describes the presentation of the entries in the Basic Repertory:

> Concerning the ordering of the items, gestures were arranged like dictionary entries, according to the labeling of their semantic core. This kind of ordering was considered to be the least flawed of all those tried, and the one which allowed the clearest cross-references. Each entry is designed to include the following information: (1) Semantic keyword (and possible specifications, as proper names or current verbal accompaniments), (2) Situation and denomination in the provisional repertoire, (3) Number of cases of codification and decodification, (4) Basic physical variants (and number of productions), (5) Contexts (of the codification test) from which the item was elicited, and number of productions, (6) Other (complementary) contexts of production of the items, and number of productions, (7) Brief verbal description of the body action (and its variants), (8) Basic meaning, (9) Verbal utterances associated with the gesture, (10) Category in the classifications undertaken, (11) Relations with other items in the repertoire, (12) Other information (conclusions, usage characteristics of the gesture, bibliographical references, etc.), (13) Designs and photographs of the item. p. 200

For number 13, each gesture (in the thesis) has a photograph of the same man in front of a brick wall doing the gesture. The photographs have no motion indicated on them, though for some entries there is a sequence of photographs of the success-ive parts of the movement. There is also a cartoon sketch of the principal part of the body used in the gesture with indications of movement.

Based on the data he obtained from his coding and decoding procedures, Payrató discusses how acts may come to be regarded as symbolic and then established in the repertory of emblematic gestures.

PAYRATÓ, Lluís
2005   Past and Present Research on Emblems in the Hispanic Tradition. Methodological
       Considerations and Future Projects
       Posted talk outline from Convegno "Gesture in the Mediterranean: Developments in Gesture
       Studies in Southern Europe," Naples, October 21–23, 2005, at
       <http://mondoailati.unical.it/didattica/archiv/easyup0506/upload/_Payrato.pdf>.

This is an overview and survey with suggestions for further research. He argues for
a study of "emblems (or autonomous gestures)" within a Spanish tradition within
Spain and Spanish-speaking Latin America (no mention is made of countries in
Africa where Spanish was an official language). He has references to many
important papers and books on that topic.

He suggests comparisons of gestures within different cultures, citing a number
of sources for documentation of the 10 that he considers, with descriptions of those.
Some of those collections, particularly Morris, Collett, Marsh, and O'Shaughnessy,
1979, have dubious reliability.

PÉREZ, Faustino
2000   *Diccionario de Gestos Dominicanos*
       Private publication by the author, Santo Domingo, Dominican Republic.
       Reprinted 2014, Advanced Reasoning Forum.

This is a collection of conventional gestures the author says are emblems. The
background of the author is described in the prologue, written by a colleague.
On pp. 27–28 Pérez gives a description of the society, culture, and background
of the people of the Dominican Republic. The gestures he describes are principally
from Santo Domingo, where, he says, the tourist industry, with many North
American visitors, has affected the gestural inventory.

Each entry has the following parts:

Title

Antecedentes y descripción
       This has a conjectured origin or comment on the nature of the
       gesture along with a description of the movement.

Cinetismo
       This describes the speed of the movement.

Repetición
       This says whether the movement is repeated or in what physical
       context the gesture is made.

Vocalización involucrada
       This lists whatever vocal sounds might be made with the gesture.

Significado(s) secudario(s)
       This lists additional meanings.

Sexo del praticante
       This says whether the gesture is done principally or entirely by men,
       by women, or both.

The descriptions of how to make the gestures are ample and clear; no illustrations or photographs are given.

There are 250 entries arranged alphabetically by a key word of the title. The title can be: one or more phrases that are, apparently, equivalent to the gesture; a description of the motion of the gesture (number 106, *El giro con la mano* = circular movement of the hand); the purpose of the gesture (number 91, *Entresacar/selecionar/elegir/escoger* = To pick out / to select / to choose / to pick out, select); or a description of an emotion (number 34, *Taparse la boca de sorpresa* = to cover the mouth in surprise).

No gestures are listed for time: past, present, future, before, after.

Some entries contain what we would probably classify as separate gestures. For example, the third entry is labeled (in accord with the idea that these are emblems):

> "It's over", "It's finished", "I don't know at all", "Nothing", "That doesn't work", "It's ready", "Now–already", "It's good now", "That's enough"[116]

In the description of how to make this gesture, Pérez says:

> The facial expression denotes a kind of resignation, of pity or weariness, etc., according to the case.[117]

If the facial expression is considered part of the gesture, as we discuss on pp. 26–27, then this listing would be for two or more gestures—we cannot tell without illustrations and clearer designations of which facial expression goes with which phrase.

This appears to be careful work which will be useful for comparative studies.

PINEDO PEYDRO, Felix-Jesus
1989 *Nuevo Diccionario Gestual Español*
    C.N.S.E., Madrid.

This is a sign-language book: in the Spanish of Latin America "gestos" means "gesture" but in Spain it is often used for what Latin Americans refer to by "señas," signs from a sign-language.

PITRÉ, Giuseppe
1889 *Usi e Costumi Credenze e Prejuidizi del Popolo Siciliano Raccolti e Descritti*
    In three volumes.
    Libreria L. Pedone Lauriel di Carol Clausen.

We have been unable to obtain a copy of the second volume of this, which contains material on Sicilian gestures. Here is a short description given by Fabio Oliveri, 2000, pp. 19–20:

---

[116] "Se acabó", "Se terminó", "No sé nada", "Nada", "No va", "Está listo", "Ya", "Ya está bueno", "Ya no más"

[117] La expressión facial denota una especie de resignación, de pena o de cansancio, etc., según el caso.

Sicilian gestures were discussed in 1889 by G. Pitré in a chapter of the second volume of "Usi e Costumi, Credenze e Pregiudizi del Popolo Siciliano". Devoid as it is of illustrations, Pitré's text runs into difficulties about describing gestures which, precisely because they are signs in non-verbal communication, resist the endeavour to describe them. Pitré is the first to be aware of this, as we see when he states that "in concluding these brief and imperfect notes, I do not conceal from myself the difficulties that will be met in comprehending some of the acts and gestures described by me, difficulties which I myself had in describing them. Often there are movements which are barely hinted at, more often than not not very noticeable, always difficult to translate into words, to make clear to those who want to know them. For this reason I had to forgo not a few gestures, which the pen cannot portray."

POYATOS, Fernando
2002 *Nonverbal Communication Across Disciplines*
    Volume 1: Culture, Sensory Interaction, Speech, Conversation
    John Benjamins Publishing Company.

In this book about non-verbal communication there is a short section called "Emblems" in which the author cites about twenty-five gestures from many cultures. He mixes together conventional and illustrative gestures. For some he cites a source; for some he gives a literary quotation to document it; others are simply stated.

RECTOR, Monica
1986 Emblems in Brazilian Culture
    in P. Bouissac, M. Herzfeld, R. Poyatos, eds. *Iconicity: Essays on the Nature of Culture;*
    Festschrift for Thomas A. Sebeok on his 65th Birthday , Stauffenberg Verlag, pp. 447-462.

After a short discussion of questions about iconicity, Rector considers the 20 gestures studied in Morris, Collet, Marsh, and O'Shaughnessy, 1979, pictures of which she reproduces. She investigates whether they are known in Brazil. She showed the drawings of the gestures to sixty Brazilians from Rio de Janiero.

> We based our questions on three different points: (1) name of gesture,
> (2) signification and (3) variations (in form and content).

In the report on her study she illustrates and discusses 27 related gestures from Brazil. She further says:

> The analysis of the twenty gestures leads us to the conclusion that there are no universal gestures, in the strict meaning of the word.

RECTOR, Monica and Aluizio R. TRINTA
1986 *Comunicação Não-Verbal: A Gestualidade Brasileira*
    Petrópolis, Brazil.

This is a book about non-verbal communication, with many references to the literature on conventional gestures and a detailed exposition of the methods of Sahnny Johnson, of Ekman and Friesen, and of Morris, Collett, Marsh, and O'Shaughnessy.

The authors include a collection of 53 different conventional gestures from Brazil. Almost all are illustrated with photographs, and the movements of each is described verbally along with the meaning and/or accompanying words. Variants of some of these are also listed, bringing the total to 61. The collection is not meant to be a complete gestuary. The authors say they chose gestures foreigners would likely misinterpret, though they include "tired" with a photo of the face of someone who looks tired.

ROSA, Leone Augusto
1929   *Espressione e Mimica*
        Ulrico Hoepli, Milano. Reprinted 2014, Advanced Reasoning Forum.

Created by an well-known artist in Italy in 1929, this collection contains 362 illustrations, each accompanied by a discussion. There is no table of contents, but an index at the back of the book lists the illustrations and discussions by their titles. The drawings and discussions are meant above all as an aid to artists. At the end of the book there are drawings of the musculature of the face.

The first part includes 144 drawings of only the face and posture of the head in the following sections:

Calm (composure)
Attention
Expressions of Thinking
Moral and Physical Pain
Anger, Rage, Threat, etc.
Pleasure, Laughter, etc.
Surprise, Astonishment, Wonder
Fear, Fright, Terror
Effort (exertion)
Vexation, Protest, etc.
Smell, Taste, and Derivatives
Disgust, Contempt, Haughtiness
Shame, Humiliation, Effrontery
Worship, Prayer
Uncertainty, Ignorance
Various Ways of Breathing
Song, Cry, Yell
Mechanics of Eating and Drinking
Sleep, Awakening, Death[118]

Though Rosa seems to think that the expressions of these are universal, or at least

---

[118] Calma; Attenzione; Espressione del Pensiero; Dolore (Morale e fisico); Collera; Ira, Minaccia, ecc.; Piacere, Riso, ecc.; Sorpresa, Stupore, Meraviglia; Paura, Spavento, Terrore; Sforzo; Stizza, Protesta, ecc.; Odorato, Gusto e Derivati; Schifo, Sprezzo, Superbia; Vergogna, Avvilimento, Sfrontatezza; Adorazione, Preghiera; Incertezza, Gnorri; Soffi Vari; Canto, Grido, Urlo; Meccanica del Mangiare e del Bere; Sonno, Risveglio, Morte.

can be universally recognized, some of the emotions we could not identify from the illustrations until we looked up their title in a dictionary. Others are illustrations of what a person is doing with his face and head (e.g., Vomiting, figure 127).

The second part illustrates gestures that involve more of the body. Each of the 218 illustrations is accompanied by one or more phrases that might be spoken with the movement or to which the gesture might be a reply. In some of the drawings there is more than one person. Movement is illustrated by dotted lines, arrows, and/or successive poses in one figure. In the introductory remarks for this part, Rosa says he drew many of these illustrations as saw them on the street. The sections are:

Pointing and Its Derivatives
Showing and Its Derivatives
Rejecting
Grasping, Squeezing
Pleasure, Affection, Joy
Moral and Physical Pain
Surprise, Wonder, Fear
Entreaty, Prayer
Impatience, Protest
Oaths, Threats
Embarrassment and Uncertainty
Warning and Related
Cordiality, Sincerity, etc.
Various[119]

Some of the expressions of the first part are revisited here to show more of the body. Some of the entries are illustrations just of what people do, as for "Orchestra Conductor" ("Direttore D'Orchestra," figures 351 to 360). Some are small dramas, such as "Suspicion-Ambush" ("Sospetto-Agguato," figure 310), which shows a man holding a candle and another advancing in front of him with a gun. But, especially in the last section, there are many conventional gestures, such as "To Drink" ("Bere," figure 156) and "Cornuto" (figure 321).

ROSE, H. A.
1919 The Language of Gesture
Folklore, vol. 30, pp. 312–315.

The author discusses 12 apparently conventional gestures of "modern India" along with several religious ones. He does not say how he knows them. He compares some of them with European gestures with explanations of the differences:

In beckoning the hand is held up, palm outwards and the fingers moved

---

[119] Indicare ed i Suoi Derivati; Mostrare ed i Suoi Derivati; Respingere e Derivati; Afferare, Stringere, ecc.; Piacere, Affetto, Gioia; Dolore (Fisico e Morale); Sorprese, Meraviglia, Paura; Invocazione, Preghiera; Impazienza, Protesta; Bestemmia, Minaccia, etc.; Imbarazzo, Incertezza; Avvertimento ed Affine; Cordialitá, Sinceritá, ecc.; Varia.

downwards and inwards—just the reverse of our gesture. But these differences are readily explicable. The Indian's palm is always much lighter than the back of his hand, so the colour of the palm must attract the attention of the person whom he wishes to call to him much more than the less conspicuous complexion of the back would do. Then the extensor muscles being weaker in all Orientals than the flexor, a great many muscular opposites occur among them: notably pulling instead of pushing a saw. p. 313

Apparently he is unaware that Italians gesture in this manner, too.

ROTH, H. Ling
1889 On Salutations
      The Journal of the Anthropological Institute of Great Britain and Ireland, vol. 19,
      pp. 164–181.

This is a comparative survey of different kinds of salutations and greetings from around the world. Though the author mentions a few of his own experiences, almost all of the descriptions of gestures and their meanings are from published reports by Western visitors to other cultures, such as Captain Cook to Tahiti. It is difficult to judge how accurate the descriptions and interpretations are since the reports are not written by natives of those cultures, and those cultures have changed a great deal since the reports were written.

SAFADI, Michaela and Carol Ann VALENTINE
1988 Emblematic Gestures among Hebrew Speakers in Israel
      International Journal of Intercultural Relations, vol. 12, pp. 327–361.

The authors test 24 gestures to see if they are emblems in Israel, suggesting that 90% agreement is necessary in order for a gesture to be classified as an emblem. The gestures are illustrated with small photographs, most of which do not show movement.

   The method, however, is disingenuous: the gestures must have been known to the authors as emblems in Israel because they speak repeatedly about the "accuracy of interpretation" and "correct interpretation" of the gestures by the subjects. So the experiment could tell the researchers only how well known these gestures are in the society, not whether the movement is indeed an emblem. But there is no reason to think that the collection of subjects is representative, even for the Jewish population.[120] Moreover, the person enacting the gestures is not a native Israeli, which might account for the preponderance of American gestures being examined.

   See also the discussion of this article on pp. 25–26 above concerning the authors' method of testing comprehension of gestures out of context and with neutral facial expression. On p. 48 above we discuss their claims about universal gestures.

---

[120] The title says the research is about native Israeli Hebrew speakers. But in the abstract to the paper they refer to them as "Jews," apparently not considering native born Hebrew-speaking Christians or Muslims to be Israelis.

SAFADI, Michaela and Carol Ann VALENTINE
1990 Contrastive Analyses of American and Arab Nonverbal and Paralinguistic Communication
 Semiotica, vol. 82, pp. 269–292.

The authors review work on gestures and say about their methodology:

> Synthesis of the foregoing systems combined with personal observation in the
> Middle East resulted in the following chart comparing American and Arab
> meanings of gestures. p. 278

We are not told where or how long the authors were resident in the "Middle East,"
nor do they make clear the area to which that term refers, nor do they say if they
speak Arabic.

The authors present a chart called "Comparison of American and Arab
Meanings of Gestures," classifying as a single gesture a movement independent of its
meaning. They divide up the list of gestures according to the part of the body that is
involved. Their list includes conventional gestures (for example, fist with thumb up
for "O.K.," p. 280), movements that are typically not usually intended to communicate (e.g., how, when, and how long one gazes at another in conversation, or hiding
behind dark glasses in conversation, p. 282), as well as some that are simply nervous
habits ("Body part: Orifices; Gesture: Cleaning, especially with fingers; American
meaning: Taboo in public; Arab meaning: irrelevant." p. 282).

SAITZ, Robert L. and Edward CERVENKA, illustrations by Mel PEKARSKY.
1972 *Handbook of Gestures: Colombia and the United States*
 2nd edition, Mouton, The Hague. This is an expanded version of *Colombian and North
 American Gestures*, Centro Colombo-American, Bogota, 1962.

This is a dictionary of Colombian and American gestures. The first edition has
drawings by Renee Bigio, which for the most part do not show facial expression.
They are replaced in the second edition by drawings by Mel Pekarsky. See our
discussion of this in Sections II.A, II.D, and III.A above.

SCHERMAN, David
1946 Speaking of Pictures . . . The French Still Talk Eloquently with their Hands
 Life, Sept. 16, 1946, pp. 12–15.

Among three series of photographs of what appear to be the use of movements as
speech markers, there are 10 photographs illustrating conventional gestures, each
accompanied by a short explanation such as "Fist makes belt tightening gesture
which means 'Times are tough'."

SCHNELLER, Raphael
1985 Heritage and Changes in the Nonverbal Language of Ethiopian Newcomers
 Israel Social Science Research, vol. 3, pp. 33–54.

The author presents a list of 19 conventional gestures with another 7 described in the
body of the text that are used by Ethiopians resident in Israel, comparing them to

gestures used by Israelis. Schneller carefully describes how he has collected the
gestures from films and pictures, from Israeli literature and eyewitnesses, and from
Ethiopian immigrants themselves, so we can have confidence that these are indeed
conventional gestures used by that group.

SCHNELLER, Raphael
1988   The Israeli Experience of Crosscultural Misunderstanding: Insights and Lessons
       In *Cross-Cultural Perspectives in Nonverbal Communication*, ed. Fernando Poyatos,
       C. J. Hogrefe, pp. 153–173.

The author gives a list of 24 emblems and 2 phrases common to Ethiopian
immigrants to Israel. The physical movement of each is described verbally and the
intended meaning is given. He then tested to see whether they could be understood
by other Israelis:

> These videotaped gestures were presented for decoding to a group of 46 college
> students, selected from 14 different cultures. p. 158

He does not say whether the gestures were presented in context, and no mention is
given of how to obtain a copy of the videotapes.

Approximately 85% of the videotaped performances were identified by the
students as gestures, i.e., symbolic movements, but only about 30% were correctly
decoded. Schneller then draws conclusions about the similarity of symbolic movements and the different meanings they have in distinct cultures.

SEBEOK, Thomas and Sahnny JOHNSON, illustrations by James T. ANDREWS,
       photographs by Camilla HARSHBARGER.
1978? *A Handbook on Nonverbal Communication for Teachers of Japanese*
       A prefinal draft.
       USOE Contract No. 300-76-0232

After great difficulty we were able to obtain a copy of this work, but it was not
complete, stopping at p. 89. Most of the discussion is about body language,
communicative postures, and wearing apparel. However, a number of conventional
gestures are described: handshaking (p. 16), getting ready to speak (p. 20), bowing
(pp. 25, 30–38), smiling (pp. 39–41), calling for a waiter (p. 52), and enough/no
(pp. 57–58). Compare Sahnny Johnson, 1979, annotated above.

SEWARD, Jack
1968   *Japanese in Action*
       John Weatherhill, Inc. 2nd edition, 1983.

The author tells us that he lived for many years in Japan and speaks Japanese
fluently. From his experience he culled 28 Japanese "signs" (pp. 42–46) that he
considers significant, all but two of which are conventional gestures. He has
comments elsewhere in the text on a few other gestures. See the quote from this
work on p. 48 (footnote 52) above.

SPARHAWK, Carol Magda Pearson
1976 *Linguistics and Gesture: An Application of Linguistic Theory to the Study of
Persian Emblems*
Ph. D. Thesis, University of Michigan.

This is a study of Persian (Iranian) emblems, carried out by an American in Tehran, Michigan, and New York. See our discussion of it on pp. 16–17 above.

STEPHENSON, Joe, Nancy PINE, Zhang LIWEI, and Xie JIAN
1993   Some Gestures Commonly Used in Nanjing, PRC
Semiotica, Vol. 95, pp. 235–259.

This is a collection of gestures from the People's Republic of China. The authors describe their methodology:

> Gestures were collected during one long session when the four authors met to record and describe gestures known to the Chinese author/informants. Gestures were at first elicited by asking questions, and by asking informants what gestures accompanied a variety of situations in everyday life. Although the informants initially reported knowing and using only a few, once they began demonstrating they provided almost 100 gestures during approximately three hours of discussion and recording. Not all gestures that were collected are included here because some did not meet criteria for inclusion.
>
> Gestures were recorded on 35-millimeter color slides, by two independent written descriptions, and by audio tape recording. Gestures are not included in this description unless all four recording methods agree as to the existence, meaning, and use of the gesture. While informants were from different parts of China, they agreed that the gestures were widely understood and in general use. Informal tests with other informants confirmed this, and as noted, many gestures were observed in everyday use.

Descriptions of the background of each author is listed at the end of the paper.
The authors list 64 gestures that seem to us to be conventional, with a few photographs. They include how the hand is used to indicate numbers up to 10. See discussions and quotes from this paper on p. 44 above.

SULGER, François
1986 *Les Gestes Verite*
Editions Sand.

This book is about body language in France. Several French conventional gestures are also discussed, but only as they supplement conversation. There is also a chapter of examples of expressions of "psychological states" and a chapter on facial expressions.

SZAROTA, Beata
2008   Qualche Riflessione Sulla Relazione fra il Significate: Natura e Classificazione dei Gesti
Quasi-Linguistici Diretti
Studia Romanica Posnaniensia, vol. 35, pp. 275–293.

Much of this paper is devoted to classifying gestures into different categories. Szarota compares Italian and Polish gestures but does not say how she knows them, though it seems she is Polish; she cites no other works for verifying her descriptions of particular gestures.

On p. 278 she discusses four temporal gestures: "past," "present," "future" for both Italy and Poland, and "after" for Italy only:

> 1. The concept of past time ("yesterday") can be expressed with the hand thrust behind the back;
> 2. Present time is indicated with the vertical position of the body.
> The concept "now" and "here" are presented with the index finger pointed downwards;
> 3. The idea of the future, that is, "tomorrow", is understood as a wavy movement from left to right, slightly thrust downward;
> 4. To indicate the concept of "after" the Italians make small circles with the hand often forward.
> The temporal deictic gestures act according to the diagrams below, that demonstrate how time is conceived:
> LEFT/RIGHT = PAST/FUTURE
> DOWN = PRESENT
> BACK/FORWARD = PAST/FUTURE
> MOVEMENT = TIME[121]

We are not told whether these gestures can be used as tenses.

Szarota also goes over 13 gestures for space and discusses a number of particular conventional gestures, illustrated with schematic line drawings with indications of movement. Her main focus, though, is on classification.

TADA, Michitaro
2004   *Japanese Gestures*
   Translated by Tomiko Sasagawa Stahl and Anna Kazumi Stahl, Three Forks Press.

This is a collection of short essays about Japanese culture written for a Japanese newspaper. Many conventional Japanese gestures are mentioned, with some discussed at length, but no descriptions are given of the movements involved nor of their specific meanings; only their role in Japanese culture is considered.

---

[121] 1. Il concetto del tempo passato ("ieri") viene espresso con la mano spinta dietro le spalle; 2. Il tempo presente è indicato con la posizione verticale del corpo. I concetti "ora" e "qui" sono presentati con l'indice teso rivolto verso il basso; 3. L'idea del futuro, cioè di "domani", è intesa come un movimento sinoidale fatto da sinistra e destra e proteso un po' in avanti; 4. Per indicare il concetto di "dopo" gli italiani fanno brevi cerchi con la mano spesso in avanti.
   I gesti deittici temporali agiscono secondo gli schemi sotto riportati, che dimostrano in quale modo venga concepito il tempo:
   SINISTRA/DESTRA = PASSATO/FUTURO;
   BASSO = PRESENTE;
   INDIETRO/DAVANTI = PASSATO/FUTURO;
   MOVIMENTO = TEMPO

TAKAGAKI, Toshihiro, Hiroto UEDA, Emma Martinell GIFRE, and María José GELABERT
1998 *Pequeño Diccionario de Gestos Españoles*
       Edition in Japanese, Tokio, Hakusuisha.

We have been unable to locate a copy of this, which we suspect is a variant of
Gelabert, Gifre, TD-Guach, and Mestre, 1990. See also Gifre and Ueda, 2002.

TSOUTSOS, Theodora M.
1970 *A Tentative Gesture Inventory for the Teaching of French*
       Master's Thesis, Queen's College, City University of New York.

Tsoutsos says she's a teacher of French to students age twelve to fourteen in New
York City. To illustrate the gestures described by Brault, 1963 (annotated above),
she photographed two of her students, one girl who had come from Paris less than
one year earlier, and one girl from Haiti who had been in the U.S. two years, noting
that these gestures are common in both countries. She gives very detailed physical
descriptions of the gestures and good explanations of how they are used, sometimes
with comparisons to American gestures that are similar in form or meaning.

Unfortunately, the photocopy of this work that is available from Queen's
College reproduces the photographs very badly.

VON GLAUNING, Captain
1904 Forms of Salutation amongst Natives of East Africa
       Journal of the Royal African Society, vol. 3, pp. 288–299.

> The following article gives a summary—I fear an incomplete one—of the forms
> taken by the greeting in a great number of races represented in the German East
> Africa Protectorate, partly from my own notes, and partly from statements of
> others. p. 288

Von Glauning describes forms of greetings which in about 20 cases involve
gestures, but whether conventional or not is difficult to determine. Many of the
descriptions are curious, for example, concerning the Wangoni:

> On specially festive occasions chiefs and Europeans are saluted by men and
> women rolling on the ground. p. 296

As to whether they are accurate, consider that he says:

> Even races which stand on the lowest step of civilization are able to express
> their thoughts amongst themselves through speech and gesture, and thus
> exchange in all their intercourse a definite greeting as a sign of friendly feeling
> towards the equal or as an expression of deference toward the superior. p. 288

WALZ, Joseph Chandler
1979 Filming French Gestures
       Foreign Language Annals, vol. 12, no. 4, pp. 285–287.

The author describes how he made a film to use in teaching French to American
students that showed 10 French conventional gestures. Here he describes verbally

the movements of the gestures, with the meaning either described, too, or given by the title of the gesture, sometimes comparing it to an American one that is similar in meaning or form. In particular, he says that Europeans start counting with their thumb, rather than with their index finger as Americans do. We do not know how to obtain a copy of the film, though he describes its contents well.

WESPI, H. U.
1949 Die Geste als Ausdrucksform und ihre Beziehungen zur Rede: Darstellung anhand von Beispielen aus der französischen Literatur zwischen 1900 und 1945. [Gestures as a Form of Expression and Their Relationship to Speech: Representation Using Examples from French Literature 1900–1945]
Romanica Helvetica, A. Francke Verlag, vol. 33, 171 pages.

This is about speech markers and expressions of emotions, particularly stylized emotions.

WIKIPEDIA
2010 *Gestures: Salute, Hitchhiking, Handshake, Roman Salute, Nazi Salute, List of Gestures, Sign of the Horns, V Sign, Mudra, Sign of the Cross*
Books LLC.

This is a printed collection of entries about gestures from Wikipedia. Published in 2010, no dates are given for when the entries were made or last updated.
Concerning the reliability of the entries, the preface to the book says:

After a long process of discussion, debate, and argument, articles gradually take on a neutral point of view reached through consensus. Additional editors expand and contribute to articles and strive to achieve balance and comprehensive coverage. . . .

Wikipedia is open to a large contributor base, drawing a large number of editors from diverse backgrounds. This allows Wikipedia to significantly reduce regional and cultural bias found in many other publications, and makes it very difficult for any group to censor and impose bias. A large, diverse editor base also provides access and breadth on subject matter that is otherwise inaccessible or little documented.

Think you can improve the book? If so, simply go to the online version and suggest changes. If accepted, your additions could appear in the next edition!

The preface is not signed, no contribution is signed, and who accepts or rejects contributions is not stated.
Here is one example:

Choking sign to indicate that one is choking is to hold the throat with one or both hands as if strangling oneself. This is recognized as a request for immediate first aid for choking. It is promoted as a way to prevent onlookers from confusing the victim's distress with some other problem, such as a heart attack, when the person cannot speak. p. 172

We have never seen or heard of this, and it seems unlikely to us that someone would have the presence of mind to do this action while actually choking. It seems that the contributor has confused doing with signifying what you are doing.

Some bias does remain in the entries. Consider:

> It is generally expected in Western culture that a male handshake should be firm. Weak handshakes are sometimes referred to as 'limp' or 'cold'. p. 125

This would be right only if by "Western culture" the contributor means mainstream white English-speaking culture in the United States and perhaps northern Europe; it's false of Mexico and among Hispanics in the United States.

When we hear or read something whose source is not named, we have no reason to accept it as accurate. As we read an extended piece, such as this collection, we expect to find some consistency in how words are used and what ideas are being explored so that we may make comparisons. We cross-check what is written in one place with another to gain not only greater understanding of what points are being made but also to gain confidence in the author's insights. The entries here, however, have no coherence, terms are used differently, and no general points are made that run throughout. Lots of ignorant people correcting each other does not result in a reliable source. At best, these entries, this book, and Wikipedia generally are useful only to stimulate our imaginations and provide references which we can consult.[122]

WISEMAN, Nicholas
1837 Review of *La mimica degli Antichi Investigata nel Gestire Napoletano*, de Jorio, 1832. *The Dublin Review*, vol. 3, no. 5, pp. 1–15.

Though Wiseman misconstrues de Jorio's work as being about speech markers, he uses the opportunity of reviewing it to describe and discuss many Italian gestures and their context of use, which he says he knows from personal experience. "In discussing this subject, we have drawn more upon our observations than upon the Canon's book, which, however, has ever been at our side, to form a corrective, when necessary, to our recollections" (p. 10). The gestures are principally, it seems, from Naples, but also Genoa and Sicily.

He also makes generalizations about them. For example, he describes the gesture of the thumb applied to the side of the nose as meaning "that the party aimed at is little better than a goose." This, he says, is meant to describe the Italian phrase *e resato con un' palmo di naso*, which he translates as "he was left with a palm's length of nose," and then says, "Almost every gesture may thus be traced to some proverbial or idiomatic phrase" (p. 5).

Throughout Wiseman compares English and Italian use of gestures, saying on p. 14, "The fingers, indeed, which are of little use to an English speaker, whose action is chiefly in the arm, are in constant use, especially in enumerating or dividing a subject."

---

122 See <http://chronicle.com/article/The-Undue-Weight-of-Truth-on/130704/> for a critique of how ignorance can trump expertise in Wikipedia. See *The New Yorker* website for the supposed expertise of editors at Wikipedia <http://www.newyorker.com/archive/2006/07/31/060731fa_fact> .

WU, Charlene
2011   Chapter Five: Nonverbal Communication Web Project
     Accessed at <http://soc302.tripod.com/soc_302rocks/id6.html> on August 24, 2011.

This is the website that convinced us to stop trying to catalogue collections of gestures on the Internet. Entries here are given by country. Here is a complete one:

MEXICO
  1. National drink in Mexico is tequila.
  4. Hands on hips is a sign of hostility.
  5. Patience is important.
  9. Women (initiate the handshake) and men greeting with a warm and soft handshake.
  10. With friends, men greet with the abrazo, a slight hug with a few pats on the back; women lightly hug and pretend to kiss the cheek.

WYLIE, Laurence and Rick STAFFORD
1977   *Beaux Gestes: A Guide to French Body Talk*
     The Undergraduate Press, Cambridge, MA and E. P. Dutton, New York.

This book contains about 67 French gestures compiled by Wylie, illustrated with photographs by Stafford of Wylie, a trained actor, performing the gesture. Wylie is dressed in a black turtleneck sweater to isolate exactly what is important in the movement. A few gestures have motion illustrated with stopgap photography.

On his methodology, Wylie writes:

> I learned many of the gestures in this book from young French actors at the Jacques Lecoq School in Paris for *Mime-Mouvement-Théâtre,* where I spent the year 1972-1973 studying cultural differences in body movement and nonverbal communication. . . .
>
> Seven French students, three women and four men, formed a sort of seminar and we spent hours at a café table making lists and definitions. Within a few days we had well over two hundred gestures. Then we went through the collection and retained those that could be clearly recognized without words and context by most French people, even though they might not use them. My colleague, Alfred Guzzetti, and I turned one of the school's practice rooms into a studio and filmed the seven students acting out the gestures. The result was a film that Guzzetti edited the following year and which we dignified with the title, *Preliminary Repertory of French Gestures.*[123]

There is very little in the book about the context in which each gesture is appropriate. Concerning the prevalence of gesturing, Wylie writes on pp. x–xi:

> Despite their reputation, the Italians do not gesture *that* much more than the French. They look more animated because of the manner in which they gesticulate.

---

[123] pp. ix–x. No reference is given for how to obtain the film. Alfred Guzzetti (private communication) says that it is a 16mm black-and-white film in two versions, one with an English sound track and the other with a French one, which he hopes to digitize.

Their movements characteristically involve the upper, as well as the lower, arm. ... The French make less use of the upper arm than the Italians but they do not press it against the ribs. ...

As for the Americans, Jacques Lecoq pointed out to me that we frequently hold our arms still and move our heads and torsos in rhythm with our words.

Part of the charm of this book are the fanciful etymologies and Freudian interpretations of gestures that Wylie gives. He is having fun, while being careful to indicate that he is only guessing in this book meant for language study in America.

See also the quote by Wylie concerning expressions of pain on p. 8 above.

Bibliography

Included here all books and articles referred to in the essay or the Annotated Bibliography.

Note: The word "gesture" in the title of a book is not an indication that it has relevance to the study of conventional gestures, e.g., Kostolany, 1977, is about body language and customs.

ACOCELLA, Joan
2000 The Neapolitan Finger
      New York Review of Books, Dec. 21, 2000, pp. 48–55.

ADAM, Meike, Wiebke IVERSEN, Erin WILKINSON, and Jill P. MORFORD
2007 Meaning on the One Hand and on the Other: Iconicity in Native vs. Foreign Signed Languages
      In E. Tabakowska, C. Ljungberg & O. Fischer, eds., *Insistent Images,* John Benjamins,
      pp. 209-225.

ADAMS, Thomas W.
1987 *Body English*: *A Study of Gestures*
      Scott, Foresman and Company.

ALSOP, Stewart
1960 How to Speak French without Saying a Word
      Saturday Evening Post, Dec. 24–31, pp. 26–29.

AMADES, Joan
1957 El Gest a Catalunya
      Annales del Instituto de Lingüistica, Universidad Nacional de Cuyo (Mendoza, Argentina),
      vol. VI, pp. 88–148.

ARMSTRONG, Nancy and Melissa WAGNER
2003 *Field Guide to Gestures: How to Identify and Interpret Virtually Every Gesture Known to Man*
      Quirk Books.

AXTELL, Roger E., illustrations by Mike FORNWALD
1991 *Gestures*: *The Do's and Taboos of Body Language around the World*
      John Wiley & Sons, Inc. Revised and expanded edition, 1998.

BACON, Albert M.
1881 *A Manual of Gesture Embracing a Complete System of Notation Together with Principles of
      Interpretation and Selections for Practice*
      S. C. Griggs and Company, Chicago.

BANKS, Ann
1974 French without Language
      Harvard Today, vol. 181, pp. 4–6.

BARAKAT, Robert A.
1969 Gesture Systems
      Keystone Folklore Quarterly, vol. 14, pp. 105–121.
1973 Arabic Gestures
      Journal of Popular Culture, vol. 6, pp. 749–787.

BASTO, Cláudio
1938 A Linguagem dos Gestos em Portugal
      Revista Lusitana, vol. 36, pp. 5–72.

BAÜML, Betty J. and Franz H. BAÜML,
1975 *A Dictionary of Gestures*
The Scarecrow Press, Inc.

BILLS, A. G.
1934 *General Experimental Psychology*
Longmans, Green.

BRAULT, Gerard J.
1963 Kinesics and the Classroom: Some Typical French Gestures
American Association of Teachers of French, vol. 36, pp. 374–382.

BREMMER, Jan and Herman ROODENBERG, eds.
1991 *A Cultural History of Gesture*
Cornell University Press.

BREWER, W. D.
1951 Patterns of Gesture among the Levantine Arabs
American Anthropologist, 1953, pp. 232–237.

BROIDE, Nitza
1977 *Israeli emblems: Israeli Communicative Units: Emblem Repertoire of
"Sabras" (Israeli natives) of Eastern European Descent*
Doctoral dissertation, University of Tel Aviv.

CALBRIS, Geneviève
1990 *The Semiotics of French Gestures*
Translated by Owen Doyle, Indiana University Press.

CALBRIS, Geneviève, Jacques MONTREDON, dessins de ZAÜ
1986 *Des Gestes et des Mots pour le dire*
Clé International.

CANGELOSI, Don and Joseph Delli CARPINI
1989 *Italian without Words*
Meadowbrook Press, Simon & Schuster.

CARDONA, Miguel
1954 Gestos o Ademanes Habituales en Venezuela
Archivos Venezolanos de Folklore (1953–1954)
Caracas, Universidade Central de Venezuela, Año II-III, tomo II, número 3, pp. 159–166.

CARMICHAEL, L., S. O. ROBERTS, and N. Y. WESSELL
1937 Study of the Judgment of Manual Expression as Presented in Still and Motion Pictures
Journal of Social Psychology, vol. 8, pp. 115–142.

CARPITELLA, Diego
1972 *Cineseca Culturales 1 Napoli*
Rome. Accessed at <www.europeanfilmgateway.eu>
???? *Cineseca Culturale 2 Babaglia*
No bibliographic data available.
1981 Cinesica 1. Napoli. Il linguaggio del Corpo e le Tradizioni Popolari: Codici Democinesici e
Ricerca Cinematografica
La Ricerca Folklorica, no. 3, Antropologia visiva. Il cinema. pp. 61–70.

CASCUDO, Luís da Câmara
1976 *Historia dos Nossos Gestos*: *Uma Pesquisa na Mímica do Brasil*
Melhoramentos. Corrected edition, Global Editora, 2003. Also in
Coleção Reconquista do Brasil, 2, vol. 104, Universidade de São Paulo, 1987.

CESTERO. *See* MANCERA, Ana Maria Cestero.

COCCHIARA, Giuseppe
1932 *Il Linguagio del Gesto*
Fratelli Boca, Torino. Published in a new edition 1977 by Sellerio editore Palermo with an
Introductory Note by Silvana Miceli .

COOKE, Jean
1959 A Few Gestures Encountered in a Virtually Gestureless Society
Western Folklore, vol. 18, pp. 233–23.

CREIDER, Chet A.
1977 Towards a Description of East African Gestures
Sign Language Studies, vol. 14 (1977), pp. 1–20.

CRITCHLEY, Macdonald
1939 *The Language of Gesture*
Edward Arnold & Co. Reprinted by The Folcroft Press Inc., 1970.

DAHAN, G. and J. COSNIER
1977 Sémiologie des Quasi-Linguistiques Français
Psychologie Médicale, vol. 9, no. 11, pp. 2053–2071.

D'ANGELO, Lou
1975 *How to Be an Italian*
Price/Stern/Sloan.

DAVIDSON, Levette
1950 Some Current Folk Gestures and Sign Language
American Speech, vol. 25, pp. 3–9.

DE JORIO, Andrea
1832/ *Gesture in Naples and Gesture in Classical Antiquity*
2000 Indiana University Press, 2000.
A translation of *La mimica degli antichi investigata nel gestire napoletano*, 1832
by Adam Kenson with an introduction by Kendon.

DEVEREUX, George
1949 Some Mohave Gestures
American Anthropologist, n.s. vol. 51, pp. 325–326.

DIADORI, Pierangela
1990 *Senza Parole* [100 Words]
Bonacci editore.

DOMINIQUE, Nilma Nascimento
2008a *Emblemas Gestuales Españoles y Brasileñas: Estudio Comparativo*
Biblioteca Virtual redELE; Red Electrónica de Didáctica del Español como Lengua Extranjera.
Accessed at <http://redined.mecd.gob.es/xmlui/bitstream/handle/11162/76274/
00820103006785.pdf?sequence=1> on August 1, 2013.

2008b Inventario de Emblemas Gestuales Españoles y Brasileños
> *Language Design*, vol. 10, pp. 5–75. Accessed at http://elies.rediris.es/Language_
> Design/LD10/LD_10_01_Nilma_Pazeado.pdf, August 7, 2013.

EASTMAN, Carol M. and Yahya Ali OMAR
1985 Swahili Gestures: Comments ("vielizi") and Exclamations ("viingizi")
> *Bulletin of the School of Oriental and African Studies, University of London*, vol. 48,
> pp. 321–332.

EFRON, David, illustrations by Stuyvesant VAN VEEN
1941/ *Gesture, Race and Culture*
1972 Mouton, The Hague. This is an expanded version of *Gesture and Environment*,
> King's Crown, New York, 1941. Spanish translation, *Gesto, Raza y Cultura*,
> Ediciones Nueva Visión, Buenos Aires, 1970.

EIBL-EIBESFELDT, I.
1972 Similarities and Differences between Cultures in Expressive Movements
> In *Non-Verbal Communication*, ed. R. A. Hinde, Cambridge University Press, pp. 297–314.

EKMAN, Paul
1976 Movements with Precise Meanings
> *Journal of Communication*, vol. 26, 14-26.
> *See also* EKMAN and FRIESEN, 1969, 1972, and JOHNSON, EKMAN, and FRIESEN, 1975.

EKMAN, Paul and Wallace V. FRIESEN
1968 Nonverbal Behavior in Psychotherapy
> In J. Schlien, ed., *Research in Psychotherapy*, vol. 3, American Psychological
> Association, pp. 179–216.
1969 The Repertoire of Nonverbal Behavior: Categories, Origins, Usage, and Coding
> *Semiotica*, vol. 1, pp. 49–98. Reprinted in Kendon, 1981c, pp. 57–105.
1972 Hand Movements
> *Journal of Communication*, vol. 22, 1972, pp. 353–374.
> *See also* JOHNSON, EKMAN, and FRIESEN, 1975.

ELGIN, Catherine Z.
1996 Index and Icon Revisited
> In *Peirce's Doctrine of Signs: Theory, Application, and Connection*, eds. V. M. Colaprieto
> and T. M. Olshewsky, Mouton de Gruyter.

EPSTEIN, Richard L.
1994 *Predicate Logic*
> Oxford University Press. Reprinted 2012, Advanced Reasoning Forum.
1998 *Critical Thinking*
> Wadsworth. 4th edition with With Michael Rooney, Advanced Reasoning Forum, 2013.
> Illustrations by Alex Raffi.
2015 The World as Process
> To appear in Epstein, *Reasoning and Formal Logic*, Advanced Reasoning Forum.
2015 Language-Thought-Meaning
> To appear in Epstein, *Reasoning and Formal Logic*, Advanced Reasoning Forum.

EPSTEIN, Richard L., Fred KROON, and William S. ROBINSON
2012 Subjective Claims
> In Epstein, *The Fundamentals of Argument Analysis*, Advanced Reasoning Forum, pp. 95–130.

FATEHI, Kamal
1996 *International Management: A Cross-Cultural Functional Perspective*
Prentice-Hall.

FELDMAN, Sandor S.
1959 *Mannerisms of Speech and Gestures in Everyday Life*
International Universities Press.

FLASCHKAMPF, Ludwig
1938 Spanische Gebärdensprache
Romanische Forschungen, vol. 52, pp. 205–258.
1939 El Lenguaje de los Gestos Españoles
Ensayos y Estudios, Berlin I/4, pp. 248–279.

FRAWLEY, William, Kenneth C. HILL, and Pamela MUNRO
2002a *Making Dictionaries: Preserving Indigenous Languages of the Americas*
University of California Press.
2002b Making a Dictionary: Ten Issues
In FRAWLEY, HILL, and MUNRO, 2002a, pp. 1–22.

GELABERT, María José and Emma Martinell GIFRE, drawings by TD-GUACH and
Josep Coll MESTRE
1990 *Diccionario de Gestos con sus Giros Más Usuales*
Edelsa, Madrid.

GIFRE, Emma Martinell and Hiroto UEDA
2002 *Diccionario de Gestos Españoles*
Versión Internet. Ver. 2002/12/8// Accessos: 4/15218,
<http://gamp.c.u.-tokyo.ac.jp/~ueda/gestos/index.html>.

GREEN, Jerald R.
1968 *A Gesture Inventory for the Teaching of Spanish*
Chilton Books, Philadelphia.

GREENBERG, Joseph H.
1957 *Essays in Linguistics*
University of Chicago Press.

GRIMES, Joseph E.
2002 Lexical Functions as a Heuristic for Huichol
In FRAWLEY, HILL, and MUNRO, 2002a, pp. 70–85.

HACKS, Charles, illustrations by Henri LANOS
1892 *Le Geste*
Marpon & Flammarion.

HAMALIAN, Leo
1965 Communication by Gesture in the Middle East
ETC.; a Review of General Semantics, vol. 22, pp. 43–49.

HAMIRU•AQUI
2004 *70 Japanese Gestures*
Translated by Alice Chang. Stone Bridge Press.

HARPER, Robert G., Arthur N. WIENS, and Joseph D. MATARAZZO
1978   Nonverbal Communication: The State of the Art
John Wiley & Sons.

HARRISON, Phyllis A.
1983   *Behaving Brazilian*
Newbury House Publishers.

HAVILAND, John B.
2003   How to Point in Zinacantán
In KITA, pp. 139–169.

HAYES, Francis C.
1940   Should We Have a Dictionary of Gestures?
Southern Folklore Quarterly, vol. 4, pp. 239–245.
1957   Gestures: A Working Bibliography
Southern Folklore Quarterly, vol. 21, pp. 218–317.

HOCKETT, C. F.
1987   *Refurbishing our Foundations: Elementary Linguistics from an Advanced Point of View*
John Benjamins Publishing Company.

INDIJ, Guido
2006   *Sin Palabras: Gestiario Argentino / Speechless: A Dictionary of Argentine Gestures*
Bilingual edition, La Marca Editora, Buenos Aires.

JAKOBSON, Roman
1972   Motor Signs for "Yes" and "No"
Language in Society, vol. 1, pp. 91–96.

JOHNSON, Harold G., Paul EKMAN, and Wallace V. FRIESEN
1975   Communicative Body Movements: American Emblems
Semiotica, vol. 15, pp. 335–353. *See also* EKMAN and FRIESEN, 1969, 1972, and EKMAN, 1976.

JOHNSON, Kenneth R.
1971   Black Kinesics—Some Non-Verbal Communication Patterns in the Black Culture
The Florida FL Reporter, vol. 9, nos. 1 and 2, ed. Alfred C. Aarons, pp. 17–20, 57.
Reprinted in *Perspectives on Black English*, J. Dillard ed., Mouton, 1975, pp. 296–306.

JOHNSON, Sahnny
1979   *Nonverbal Communication in the Teaching of Foreign Languages*
Ph.D. Thesis, Indiana University.

JOSEPH, Jason and Rick JOSEPH
2007   *101 Ways to Flip the Bird*
Broadway Books.

KANNER, L.
1931   Judging Emotions from Facial Expressions
Psychological Monographs, 1931, vol. 41, no. 18, pp. 1–91.

KANY, Charles E.
1960   *American-Spanish Euphemisms*
University of California Press.

KAULFERS, Walter Vincent
1931 Curiosities of Colloquial Gestures
Hispania, Vol. 14, pp. 249–264.
1932 A Handful of Spanish
Education, vol. 52, pp. 423–428.

KENDON, Adam
1981a Geography of Gesture
Essay review of MORRIS, COLLETT, MARSH, and O'SHAUGHNESSY, 1979.
Semiotica, vol. 37, pp. 129–163.
1981b Introduction: Current Issues in the Study of "Nonverbal Communication"
In Kendon, 1981c, pp. 1–53.
1981c *Nonverbal Communication, Interaction, and Gesture*
Adam Kendon, ed., Approaches to Semiotics 41, Mouton (The Hague).
1984 Did Gesture Have the Happiness to Escape the Curse at the Confusion of Babel?
In *Nonverbal Behavior: Perspectives, Applications, Insights*, ed. Aaron Wolfgang,
C. J. Hogrefe, Inc., pp. 76–114.
1987 Gestures
In *Gallaudet Encyclopedia of Deaf People and Deafness*, ed. J. V. Van Cleve, vol. 1 (A–G),
McGraw-Hill, 1987.
1992 Abstraction in Gesture
Essay review of CALBRIS, 1990. *Semiotica*, vol. 90, pp. 225–250.
2000 Introduction to DE JORIO, 1832/2000.
2004 *Gesture: Visible Action as Utterance*
Cambridge University Press.

KEY, Mary
1962 Gestures and Responses: A Preliminary Study Among Some Indian Tribes of Bolivia
Studies in Linguistics, vol. 16, pp. 92–99.

KING, W.
1949 Hand Gestures
Western Folklore, vol. 8, pp. 263–264 (in the section "Notes and Queries").

KIRK, Lorraine and Michael BURTON
1976 Physical versus Semantic Classification of Nonverbal Forms: A Cross-Cultural Experiment
Semiotica, vol. 17. Reprinted in Kendon, 1981c, pp. 459–481.

KITA, Sotaro, ed.
2003 *Pointing: Where Language, Culture, and Cognition Meet*
Lawrence Erlbaum Associates, Publishers.

KOSTOLANY, F.
1977 *Los Gestos*
Mensajero, Bilbao. Originally published as *Les Gestes*, Centre d'Étude et de Promotion
de la Lecture, Paris.

KRISTEVA, J. and M. LACOSTE
1968 Bibliographie
Pratiques et Langages Gestuels, No. 10, Juin, 1968, pp. 132–149.

LABARRE, Weston
1947 The Cultural Basis of Emotions and Gestures
      Journal of Personality, vol. 16, pp. 49–69.

LEITE DE VASCONCELLOS, J., illustrations by Saavedra MACHADO
1917 A Linguagem de Gestos
      Alma Nova, vol. 22, no. 21–24. Published as a separate volume by Imprensa de Manuel Lucas
      Torres, Lisboa.

LEONE, Jay
1992 *Italian without Words: An Illustrated Guide to Italian Hand Gestures*
      S.P.I. Books.

LYONS, John
1971 *Introduction to Theoretical Linguistics*
      Cambridge University Press.

MALLERY, Garrick
1880 *Sign Language among North American Indians Compared with that among Other Peoples
      and Deaf-Mutes*
      U. S. Bureau of American Ethnology, Smithsonian Institution, Annual Report, vol. 1,
      1879–1880, pp. 263–552. Reprinted 2011, Dover Publications.

MANCERA, Ana María Cestero
1999a *Comunicación No Verbal y Ensenza de Lengua Extranjeras*
      Arco/Libros, S. L., Madrid.
1999b *Repertorio Básico de Signos No Verbales del Español*
      Arco/Libros, S. L., Madrid.

MARTIN, Peter
2003 How to Tell the French to Screw Off
      Esquire, July, p. 24.

McCORD, Charlotte
1948 Gestures
      Western Folklore, vol. 7, pp. 290–292.

McNEILL, David
1992 *Hand and Mind: What Gestures Reveal about Thought*
      The University of Chicago Press.
1998 Speech and Gesture Communication
      In J. M. Iverson and S. Goldin-Meadow, eds., *The Nature and Function of Gestures in
      Children's Communication*, Jossey-Bass Publishers, pp. 11–27.

MEISSNER, Martin and Stuart B. PHILPOTT, illustrated by Diana PHILPOTT
1975 A Dictionary of Sawmill Workers' Signs
      Sign Language Studies vol. 9, pp. 309- 347.

MEO-ZILIO, Giovanni
1960 Consideraciones Generales sobre el Languaje de los Gestos
      Boletâin de Filologia (Universidade de Chile, Santiago de Chile), XII, pp. 225-248.
      See also MEO-ZILIO, 1989.
1961a El Lenguaje de los Gestos en Uruguay
      Boletâin de Filologia (Universidade de Chile, Santiago de Chile), XIII, pp. 75–163.
      See also MEO-ZILIO, 1989.

1961b *El Lenguaje de los Gestos en el Río de la Plata*
    Imp. Libertad, Montevideo. (This is Meo-Zilio, 1960 and Meo-Zilio, 1961 with the
    addition of a bibliography.)
1986 El Lenguaje de los Gestos en el Dominio Hispanófono: Comportamientos Morfosintácticos y
    Derivacionales
    In *Actas del VIII Congreso Internacional de la Asociación de Hispanistas* (Providence, 1983),
    Ediciones Istmo, Madrid, pp. 305–315.
1989 *Estudios Hispanoamericanos: Temas Lingüísticos*
    Bulzoni Editore, Roma.
    This contains revised versions of Meo-Zilio, 1960, Meo-Zilio, 1961, and Meo-Zilio, 1986.
1990a Gestos Eróticos en el Dominio Hispánico
    In *Les Langues Néo-Latines*, Paris, no. 274, fascicule 3, pp. 83-98.
1990b Gestos de Procedencia Italiana en el Plata
    Rio de la Plata, Paris, vol. 10, 1990, pp. 83–95.

MEO-ZILIO, Giovanni and J. COSNIER
1987 Expresiones 'Linguísticas' Concomitantes con Expresiones Gestuales em España e
    Hispanoamerica
    Diálogos Hispánicos de Amsterdam, vol. 6, pp. 65-79.

MEO-ZILIO, Giovanni and Silvia MEJÍA
1980- *Diccionário de Gestos: España e Hispanoamérica*
1983 Vol. I, 1980, and Vol. II, 1983. Instituto Caro y Cuervo Yerbabuena, Bogotá, Colombia.

MITTON, A.
1949 La Langage par Gestes
    Nouvelle Revue des Traditions Populaire, vol. 1, pp. 138–151.

MONAHAN, Barbara
1983 *A Dictionary of Russian Gesture*
    Hermitage, Ann Arbor, Michigan.

MORRIS, Desmond
1977 *Manwatching: A Field Guide to Human Behavior*
    Harry N. Abrams, Inc.
1994 *Bodytalk: The Meaning of Human Gestures*
    Crown Trade Paperbacks.

MORRIS, Desmond, Peter COLLETT, Peter MARSH, and Marie O'SHAUGHNESSY
1979 *Gestures: Their Origins and Distribution*
    Jonathan Cape.
    SEE also KENDON, 1981A.

MORSBACH, Helmut
1973 Aspects of Nonverbal Communication in Japan
    The Journal of Nervous and Mental Disease, vol. 157, pp. 262–277.
1988 Nonverbal Communication and Hierarchical Relationships: The Case of Bowing in Japan
    In *Cross-Cultural Perspectives in Nonverbal Communication*, ed. Fernando Poyatos,
    C.J. Hogrefe, pp. 189–199.

MUNARI, Bruno
1963 *Supplemento al Dizionario Italiano*
    Muggiani Editore Milano. Reprinted 2002 Corriani Editore.

NAPOLI, Donna Jo
2003   *Language Matters*
       Oxford University Press.

NASCIMENTO. *See* DOMINIQUE, Nilma Nascimento.

NISSET, Luc
2007   *French in Your Face!*
       McGraw-Hill.

OLIVERI, Fabio, illustrations by Jasmin CARNABUCI
2000   *La Gestualità dei Siciliani*
       2nd edition, KREA.

PAPPAS, William
1972   *Instant Greek*
       Erminoni Argolis, Greece. 12th edition published in 1999 by Chetwynd Stapylton, USA.

PAURA, Bruno and Marina SORGE, drawings by Alessia CIANFLONE
1999   *Comme te l'Aggia Dicere?   Ouvere l'arte gestuale a Napoli*
       The Art of Gestures in Naples—L'Art des Gestes à Naples—El Arte de los Gestos en Nápoles
       Edizioni Intra Moenia.

PAYRATÓ, Lluis
1989   Assaig de Dialectologia Gestual: Aproximació Pragmàtica al Repetori Bàsic d'Emblemes
       del Català de Barcelona
       Ph.D. Thesis, University of Barcelona.
1989   Comunicació No Verbal, Tipologies del Gest i Gest *Autònom*
       Annuario de Filologia (Universidad de Barcelona), vol. 11–12 (1985), pp. 145–174.
1993   A Pragmatic View on Autonomous Gestures: A First Repetoire of Catalan Emblems
       Journal of Pragmatics, vol. 20, pp. 193–216.
2005   Past and Present Research on Emblems in the Hispanic Tradition. Methodological
       Considerations and Future Projects
       Posted talk outline from Convegno "Gesture in the Mediterranean: Developments in Gesture
       Studies in Southern Europe," Naples, October 21–23, 2005, at
       <http://mondoailati.unical.it/didattica/archiv/easyup0506/upload/_Payrato.pdf>. Accessed 2010.

PÉREZ, Faustino
2000   *Diccionario de Gestos Dominicanos*
       Private edition by the author, Santo Domingo, Dominican Republic. Published 2014,
       Advanced Reasoning Forum.

PINEDO PEYDRO, Felix-Jesus
1989   *Nuevo Diccionario Gestual Español*
       C.N.S.E., Madrid.

PITRÉ, Giuseppe
1889   *Usi e Costumi Credenze e Prejuidizi del Popolo Siciliano Raccolti e Descritti*
       In three volumes.
       Libreria L. Pedone Lauriel di Carol Clausen.

POGGI, Isabella and Marina ZOMPARELLI
1987   Ipotesi sul Lessico dei Gesti
       In P. E. Ricci Bitti, ed., *Communicazione e Gestualità*, Franco Angeli Libri., pp. 134–158.

POLING, Tommy H.
1978 Sex Differences, Dominance, and Physical Attractiveness in the Use of Nonverbal Emblems
       Psychological Reports, vol. 43, pp. 1087–1092.

POYATOS, Fernando
1975 Gesture Inventories: Fieldwork Methodology and Problems
       Semiotica, vol. 13, pp. 199–227. Reprinted in Kendon, 1981C, pp. 371–399.
2002 *Nonverbal Communication Across Disciplines*
       Volume 1: Culture, Sensory Interaction, Speech, Conversation
       John Benjamins Publishing Company.

QUINE, Willard Van Orman
1960 *Word and Object*
       The M. I. T. Press.

RABANALES, Ambrosio
1955 La Somatolalia [Body Language]
       Boletâin de Filologia (Universidade de Chile, Santiago), vol. VIII (1954–1955), pp. 355–378.

RECTOR, Monica
1986 Emblems in Brazilian Culture
       in P. Bouissac, M. Herzfeld, R. Poyatos, eds. *Iconicity: Essays on the Nature of Culture;
       Festschrift for Thomas A. Sebeok on his 65th Birthday*, Stauffenberg Verlag, pp. 447-462.

RECTOR, Monica and Aluizio R. TRINTA
1986 *Comunicação Não-Verbal: A Gestualidade Brasileira*
       Petrópolis, Brazil.

RICCI BITTI, Pio Enrico and Isabella POGGI
1991 Symbolic Nonverbal Behavior: Talking through Gestures
       In *Fundamentals of Nonverbal Behavior*, eds. Robert S. Feldman and Bernard Rimé,
       Cambridge University Press and Editions de la Maison des Sciences de l'Homme, pp. 443–457.

ROSA, Leone Augusto
1929 *Espressione e Mimica*
       Ulrico Hoepli, Milano. Reprinted 2014, Advanced Reasoning Forum.

ROSE, H. A.
1919 The Language of Gesture
       Folklore, vol. 30, pp. 312–315.

ROTH, H. Ling
1889 On Salutations
       The Journal of the Anthropological Institute of Great Britain and Ireland, vol. 19,
       pp. 164–181.

SAFADI, Michaela and Carol Ann VALENTINE
1988 Emblematic Gestures among Hebrew Speakers in Israel
       International Journal of Intercultural Relations, vol. 12, pp. 327–361.
1990 Contrastive Analyses of American and Arab Nonverbal and Paralinguistic Communication
       Semiotica, vol. 82, pp. 269–292.

SAITZ, Robert L. and Edward CERVENKA, illustrations by Mel PEKARSKY.
1972 *Handbook of Gestures: Colombia and the United States*
       2nd edition, Mouton, The Hague.

This is an expanded version of *Colombian and North American Gestures*, Centro Colombo-American, Bogota, 1962, with illustrations by Renee Bigio.

SCHEFLEN, Albert E.
1964   The Significance of Posture in Communication Systems
       Psychiatry, vol. 27, pp. 316–331.

SCHERMAN, David
1946   Speaking of Pictures . . . The French Still Talk Eloquently with Their Hands
       Life, Sept. 16, 1946, pp. 12–15.

SCHMITT, Jean-Claude
1991   The Rationale of Gestures in the West: Third to Thirteenth Centuries
       In BREMMER and ROODENBERG, pp. 59–70.

SCHNELLER, Raphael
1985   Heritage and Changes in the Nonverbal Language of Ethiopian Newcomers
       Israel Social Science Research, vol. 3, pp. 33–54.
1988   The Israeli Experience of Crosscultural Misunderstanding: Insights and Lessons
       In *Cross-Cultural Perspectives in Nonverbal Communication*, ed. Fernando Poyatos,
       C.J. Hogrefe, pp. 153–173.

SEBEOK, Thomas and Sahnny JOHNSON, illustrations by James T. ANDREWS,
       photographs by Camilla HARSHBARGER
1978? *A Handbook on Nonverbal Communication for Teachers of Japanese*
       A prefinal draft. USOE Contract No. 300-76-0232. *See also* JOHNSON.

SEWARD, Jack
1968   *Japanese in Action*
       John Weatherhill, Inc. 2nd edition, 1983.

SHERZER, Joel
1972   Verbal and Non-Verbal Deixis: The Pointed Lip Gesture among the San Blas Cuna
       Language in Society, vol. 2, pp. 117–131.
1991   The Brazilian Thumbs-Up Gesture
       Journal of Linguistic Anthropology, vol. 1, pp. 189–197.

SPARHAWK, Carol Magda Pearson
1976   *Linguistics and Gesture: An Application of Linguistic Theory to the Study of Persian Emblems*
       Ph.D. Thesis, University of Michigan.
1978   Contrastive-Identification Features of Persian Gesture
       Semiotica, vol. 24, pp. 49–86. Reprinted in Kendon, 1981C, pp. 421–458.

STEPHENSON, Joe, Nancy PINE, Zhang LIWEI, and Xie JIAN
1993   Some Gestures Commonly Used in Nanjing, PRC
       Semiotica, Vol. 95, pp. 235–259.

SULGER, François
1986   *Les Gestes Verite*
       Editions Sand.

SZAROTA, Beata
2008   Qualche Riflessione Sulla Relazione fra il Significate: Natura e Classificazione dei Gesti
       Quasi-Linguistici Diretti
       Studia Romanica Posnaniensia, vol. 35, pp. 275–293.

TADA, Michitaro
2004 *Japanese Gestures*
Translated by Tomiko Sasagawa Stahl and Anna Kazumi Stahl, Three Forks Press.

TAKAGAKI, Toshihiro, Hiroto UEDA, Emma Martinell GIFRE, and María José GELABERT
1998 *Pequeño Diccionario de Gestos Españoles*
Edition in Japanese, Tokio, Hakusuisha.

TSOUTSOS, Theodora M.
1970 *A Tentative Gesture Inventory for the Teaching of French*
Master's Thesis, Queen's College, City University of New York.

TURULL, Antoni
1983 Review of Meo-Zilio and Mejía, 1980-1983.
Thesaurus, Instituto Caro y Cuervo, vol. 38, pp. 628–631.

VON GLAUNING, Captain
1904 Forms of Salutation amongst Natives of East Africa
Journal of the Royal African Society, vol. 3, pp. 288–299.

WALZ, Joseph Chandler
1979 Filming French Gestures
Foreign Language Annals, vol. 12, no. 4, pp. 285–287.

WASHABAUGH, William
1980 The Manu-facturing of a Language
Semiotica, vol. 29, 1980, pp. 1–37.

WESPI, H. U.
1949 Die Geste als Ausdrucksform und ihre Beziehungen zur Rede: Darstellung anhand von Beispielen aus der französischen Literatur zwischen 1900 und 1945
Romanica Helvetica, A. Francke Verlag, vol. 33, 171 pages.

WIENER, Morton, Shannon DEVOE, Stuart RUBINOW, and Jesse GELLER
1972 Nonverbal Behavior and Nonverbal Communication
Psychological Review, vol. 79, no. 3, pp. 185–214.

WILCOX, Sherman
2004 Cognitive Iconicity: Conceptual Spaces, Meaning, and Gesture in Signed Languages
Cognitive Linguistics, vol. 15, issue 2, 2004, pp. 119–147.

WIKIPEDIA
2010 *Gestures: Salute, Hitchhiking, Handshake, Roman Salute, Nazi Salute, List of Gestures, Sign of the Horns, V Sign, Mudra, Sign of the Cross*
Books LLC.

WILKINS, David
2003 Why Pointing with the Index Finger is Not a Universal (in Sociocultural and Semiotic Terms)
In KITA, pp. 171–215.

WISEMAN, Nicholas
1837 Review of *La mimica degli Antichi Investigata nel Gestire Napoletano*, de Jorio, 1832.
The Dublin Review, vol. 3, no. 5, pp. 1–15.

WU, Charlene
2011 Chapter Five: Nonverbal Communication Web Project
Accessed at <http://soc302.tripod.com/soc_302rocks/id6.html> on August 24, 2011.

WYLIE, Laurence and Rick STAFFORD
1977   *Beaux Gestes*: *A Guide to French Body Talk*
    The Undergraduate Press, Cambridge, MA and E. P. Dutton, New York.

General Bibliographies

Understanding Body Movement: *An Annotated bibliography*
    Martha Davis, Arno Press, 1972.

Body Movement and Nonverbal Communication: *An Annotated Bibliography, 1971–1981*
    Martha Davis and Janet Skupien, Indiana University Press, 1982.

Pour une Sémiologie du Geste en Afrique Occidental
    Céline Mathon, *Semiotica*, vol. 3, 1969, pp. 245–255.

Additions to the Annotated Bibliography
See www.AdvancedReasoningForum.org/gestures for updates to this Annotated Bibliography .

Index

- Names of gestures that can be found in our gestuary are listed in *italics*.
- <u>Underlined</u> page numbers indicate a quotation by the person listed.
- Numbers in parentheses indicate the pages of the cited section.
- n indicates a footnote.

www.ingramcontent.com/pod-product-compliance
Lightning Source LLC
Chambersburg PA
CBHW080757300326
41914CB00055B/923